Brenda and Eric provide a fun, user-friendly, and effective look at what's collecting in your life, and offer a pathway to freedom from the physical, virtual, and mental STUFF weighing you down. **Their personal stories make it seem they are walking alongside you as a friend.** If you want to live Clutter-Free, this book is for you!

> Carol Peters, MD, DMin, Host
> *Dr Carol Show* www.drcarolshow.com

Brenda and Eric present an interesting and **compelling book on clutter**. I admire their passion, and **their expertise comes through**.

> Brooks Palmer, Author
> *Clutter Busting*

What a wonderful feeling of surprise and wonder I felt as I finished *STUFFology 101*. Just like the cover illustration, **the pages of this book open up a world of possibility with whimsical, humorous, and poignant stories.**

For people who clutter, *STUFFology 101* offers a gentle escape from the prison of "more." What struck me most profoundly was: **What really matters?** Is it the stacks of papers teetering on tables, boxes filled with more stuff, hand-me-downs that clutter the garage, attic, and rooms of your home or is it the heart connections we have with people that matter?

**Like the occasional great teachers we had in school, Brenda and Eric inspired me to think, feel, reflect and, above all, act.** I am empowered now to face the clutter and clean up that "POOP!"

**Thank you for this book that fills a gap in the literature regarding clutter.** There is a place for *STUFFology 101* between all the books on clutter busting, feng shui, and the scientific literature on this complex and potentially crippling topic.

Patrick Arbore, EdD, Program Director
*Institute on Aging*

**Is too much clutter hiding the true value of your home?** Real estate agents are often faced with a Seller's possessions making it difficult for potential Buyers to envision themselves in the Seller's home. The process of de-cluttering can be overwhelming to the best of us. *STUFFology 101* **provides realtors with a framework** for dealing with clients with compassion in order to present their home in the best possible light.

Barbara Benchoff, Broker Associate
*Centennial Realty Group*

# STUFFology 101

## Get Your Mind Out of the Clutter

Brenda Avadian, MA
Eric M. Riddle

North Star Books
Pearblossom, CA

ISBN 978-0-9632752-5-7 (paperback edition)
ISBN 978-0-9632752-7-1 (ebook edition)

Library of Congress Cataloging-in-Publication Data

Avadian, Brenda.
 Stuffology 101 : get your mind out of the clutter / Brenda Avadian, MA, Eric Riddle.
    pages cm
 Includes bibliographical references and index.
 ISBN 978-0-9632752-5-7 (pbk.)
1. Orderliness. 2. Time management. 3. House cleaning. 4. Distraction (Psychology) I. Title.
 BJ1533.O73A93 2014
 646.7—dc23

                           2014003437

**North Star Books**
P. O. Box 589
Pearblossom, California 93553 U.S.A.
Telephone: 661-944-1130
Email: NSB@NorthStarBooks.com

*For all who*
*want to stop STUFF*
*from draining*
*their life force,*
*their energy,*
*and their vibrancy.*

*For all who*
*don't want clutter*
*to take away*
*from the time they spend*
*with people.*

# Warning-Disclaimer

# Contents

# Preface

Research shows that after our basic needs are met—and a *little* more—we are *not* happier with more stuff.

After years of conspicuous consumption—and the hunt for bigger and more things—we have finally said, "Enough!"

You won't find us featured on reality TV shows about hoarding, yet we are among those who deal with something insidious. Unlike hoarders, we live in the shadows, struggling with a lifetime of clutter. Our clutter is not compelling enough to be seen on national TV but it does affect our lives severely; diverting us from our life's purpose and what we deserve.

Out of public view, in closets and spare bedrooms, we hide stacked boxes, piles of overwhelming paperwork, and collectibles.

We are among those who still have stuff stored in boxes from our last move—even if it was ten years ago.

We wander at the "edge of the road," trying to get our minds out of the clutter.

We are among those who park our cars outside, because there is no room in the garage.

We make piles after our paperwork grows too much—piles that we scoop up and place out of sight when there's a knock on the door.

We need to go on a "clutter diet." We need to look at all of our stuff and define what clutter is in order to rid ourselves of it.

If any of this is true for you, then we, the authors, invite you to join the millions living in the shadows for whom this book was written.

We will be your guides on this journey through the land of STUFF. We are a married couple (not to each other), who share a combined eighty-three years of experience in dealing with clutter. Brenda started accumulating at age eight, Eric at age eleven. We have faced the emotional struggle of dealing with clutter. Want to know a secret? *It's an ongoing process.* We know that managing clutter is not a one-weekend or even a three-month endeavor. It may take much longer.

We've needed to be patient and understanding when dealing with our stuff, and our experience has taught us to be flexible while navigating through it.

What finally motivated us to de-clutter was when we realized that instead of doing what we wanted to do, like spending time with *people*, we were spending time with *things*. At the end of our lives, *things* won't bring us comfort, *people* will.

This book is for people who are ready to face the stuff that clutters their lives. *STUFFology 101* provides flexible tools to help get your mind out of the clutter. The steps you take to manage your own stuff will serve you when helping others deal with their stuff.

# Part One:

# STUFFology 101

Stuff, Stuff, and more STUFF!

# I Can't Park My Car in the Garage

Eric, a fan of *Green Eggs and Ham,* was inspired to write this Dr. Seuss-style poem about all of the stuff in his garage:

*Been there, done that*
*"Bin" there, why's that?*

*Whose bins are those, they're in my way*
*They are Susi's; I'd have to say*
*Keepsake clothes for babies and her*
*Throw them out and I'm dead for sure*
*Seven, eight, nine, and more*
*Not enough space for this garage to store*
*Speechless I am. What about you?*
*Can't say much because I have keepsakes too*
*Mementos of track, running shirts, and such*
*But mine is just one bin, not too much*

*Other items are here as well*
*Too much stuff it looks like hell*
*Tucked away in the garage where no one can see*
*Christmas stuff that's bugging me*
*Feeling boxed in from the holiday*

*It ends up in my garage because Susi got her way*
*Keeping it for now, must be fate*
*She will need it next year to decorate*
*Christmas junk and Easter too*
*She wants to keep it, what can I do?*

*Will I ever be able to park a car in here?*
*Not gonna happen with that trailer near*
*What's up with that trailer in this space?*
*I might need it again, just in case*
*Trailer trash that no one can see*
*Get rid of some stuff that is the key*
*But what should go and what can stay?*
*I wonder what it's worth on eBay*
*Keep it all and tell a tale*
*Of why our memories are not for sale*

# 1. What is Stuff?

"Well, there's your stuff and my stuff," said the late comedian George Carlin in a sketch titled "Stuff."[1] Some stuff matters a lot. That's because it's *our* stuff. Other stuff matters little. That's because it's *other people's* stuff.

We'll focus on the stuff that matters a lot—the stuff we can do something about—*our* stuff.

## What is stuff?

Stuff is what we've accumulated during the course of living, working, and playing day to day. During the past two decades, stuff has morphed into the virtual realm. We now store music, photos, documents, and videos on our computers and even in the cloud.

There's also the stuff between our ears. What's in our minds (our attitude) will determine how we navigate through life. Many books have been written about this. Some of these books are on our bookshelves or stored in our digital eBook readers. What we accumulate in our minds will fill us with hope, wonder, and lead us to success—*or* it will fill us with overwhelm and worry *because there's too much stuff!*

For our use here, stuff is divided into two categories—the stuff we need and use regularly and that makes our lives more comfortable (toothbrush, toilet paper, clothes, utensils, furniture, computer/tablet/smartphone, etc.) and the stuff we *think* we need and will use someday (old car, clothes that don't fit, paperwork we haven't looked at in decades, etc.).

## What is clutter?

The stuff we think we'll need someday often gets in the way—and this is what we call clutter. Whether physical clutter or mental, it's the stuff we trip over while trying to get to what we need.

The magazines we're currently reading are not clutter; whereas, the growing piles of back issues that we're trying to find the time to read are clutter.

The boxes and overstuffed shelves of seasonal decorations in the garage are not clutter until our fingertips freeze while scraping ice off the windshield of our car parked outside.

Hundreds of emails flooding our inboxes that await our reply are clutter.

# 1. What is Stuff?

Not being able to play a game of pool because it takes a half day to move the piles of stuff off the pool table are clutter.

My husband's tools are clutter.

My wife's collection of baby clothes is clutter.

Your married child's stuff still in your home is clutter.

Feeling overwhelmed after overscheduling our lives is clutter.

Too much noise is clutter.

Being stuck and not knowing why we're holding onto something adds to the clutter. "Just because" is not a good enough reason to hold on.

Oh, and finding $100,000 between two books on a living room shelf is definitely *not* clutter.

Clutter is different for each of us. The former First Lady of the Philippines, Imelda Marcos, boasted a collection of 3,000 pairs of shoes while prolific author Danielle Steele, enjoys a collection of 6,000 pairs. Most likely, these women do not consider their collections clutter; yet, it would take Steele more than sixteen years to wear a different pair of shoes each day.

Although many of us are overwhelmed if we have more than a dozen pair of shoes, sandals, boots, and slippers in our closets, we don't advocate the popular mantra: Let go of anything you have not used in a year.

Brenda stored an oriental wool rug in her bedroom closet for seventeen years because the colors didn't coordinate with the house she was living in. After she moved and redecorated, she's thankful she saved it, to enjoy it once again.

Heck, we admit to saving and now wearing certain clothes from almost thirty years ago. They're back in style and of higher quality!

Clutter is not the same as hoarding, which affects two to five percent of the population, according to Frost and Steketee, authors of *Stuff: Compulsive Hoarding and the Meaning of Things*.[2] Hoarding, once classified as Obsessive Compulsive Disorder (OCD), is now distinguished from OCD in the new *Diagnostic and Statistical Manual* as a disorder causing distress and disability among those whose homes are almost uninhabitable.[3]

## Then what is clutter?

Clutter is what blocks us from fulfilling our purpose and goals. It could be a pile of papers, too many boxes, worries, noise, too many scheduled activities, or not enough time.

# 2. Cluttergories

For an organized look at clutter, we have divided the stuff that causes us to stumble or blocks us from reaching our goals into five categories. We call these *cluttergories*.

1. Physical
2. Mental
3. Digital
4. Temporal
5. Sensual

## I. PHYSICAL

Physical clutter is what we think of most often when describing stuff that gets in the way. It deals with the material things that block our path; the things we trip over. Examples include:

- Piles of clothes that become a toxic reminder of years gone by when we weighed less

- Boxes of paperwork in the home office that remind us of years of hard work that went unappreciated
- STAR TREK memorabilia that crowd the space around the pool table
- No space to park even one car in the garage
- Too many books to read in one's lifetime

*What is getting in your way of making progress today?*

# 2. MENTAL

Mental clutter is when our minds are so occupied with thoughts we stumble as we try to move forward. Mental clutter includes *if–then* comments. *If I can just get through this, then I'll …*

Clutter of the mind includes emotions, regrets, and worries that drain us.

A school of Zen Buddhism[4] teaches that clearing one's mind of all thought is necessary before enlightenment can occur. You may have seen a master pour tea for the student until the cup overflows onto the saucer and spills onto the floor. The master then explains to the puzzled student that the mind must first be empty to fill it with teachings.

*How do we translate this in the modern world?*

Until we go on an information diet, our teacup will be flowing over.

## 2. Cluttergories

Mental clutter prevents restful slumber when our minds are too busy.

Some of us can't even take a vacation without thinking about work. We remain tethered to our jobs with smartphones and tablets.

Many of our emotions are triggered by our possessions. Popular TV shows, like *Hoarders*, feature the mental issues people have because of physical clutter. Many of us can tell a story about each item we possess—how we acquired it, when, and what it means to us. We don't want to throw away our memories; yet new thoughts can't take root in a weed-filled mind.

---

*Many of our emotions are triggered by our possessions.*

---

Mental clutter is when the ghosts of opportunities past (regrets) cause us to hold onto things (physical stuff) and thoughts (emotional baggage) that no longer serve us.

Because we're not yet ready to deal with our emotions and regrets, we procrastinate, which weighs us down and stops us from doing the things we want to do. This leads to tasks undone, which is toxic and places greater stress on our lives.

# 3. DIGITAL

Digital clutter refers to anything in virtual form. Electronic media, such as emails, photos, and music files, crowd our computer hard drives, smartphones, and tablets. We store photos on the cloud and use social media such as Facebook, Twitter, LinkedIn, and Google+.

Since hard drives have Terabyte (1,000 Gigabyte) storage capacities, we're fooled into thinking we can store tens of thousands of photos or thousands of music files because they don't require extra physical space. Yet, how many of us organize all our photos and can find what we need when we need it? With cloud computing, it gets worse.

*Can you easily locate that funny photo of you and your friends on vacation from five years ago?*

*Why are you saving all of those emails? Will you really refer to them someday? Will you be able to find the one you need?*

# 4. TEMPORAL

We experience temporal clutter when our days are filled with distractions and we focus on things that don't matter. Temporal clutter relates to physical clutter when our stuff takes so much of our time that we spend less time with people.

## 2. Cluttergories

*What are the most joyful moments of your life?* Is it when you spend time going through your stuff or when you enjoy the company of people?

When you feel your time is limited, look at your daily activities. Sometimes we fill our lives with activities and feel overwhelmed by how busy we are.

Many of us can't make time for solitude—time to think and reflect.

*Are you reaching your goals?*

*Do you have days when you are really busy—and yet, at the end of the day, you wonder what you accomplished?*

People experiencing temporal clutter often say they are too busy.

Being *busy* does not equal being *productive*.

Temporal clutter also relates to mental clutter. Procrastination joins worry in keeping our minds diverted from our goals.

We spend a lot of time and energy worrying about all the stuff we need to do. If we simply took a few minutes each day, we'd get it done in less time than we spend *thinking* about it.

All of us have 168 hours each week. How we fill those hours determines the quality of our lives.

---

*If we simply take a few minutes each day, we'd get it done in less time than we spend thinking about it.*

---

# 5. SENSUAL

Sensual clutter is when we fill our lives with too much stimuli. Brenda writes: For almost a decade, I've lived in a rural area of Los Angeles. I enjoy dark skies and quiet nights, except for a hooting owl or a howling pack of coyotes. In the summer, I hear the chorus of different insects.

When I visit my cousin's Marina City condominium in Chicago[5], I can't get to sleep. There are too many lights and too much traffic noise. I need earplugs. During the day, walking along Michigan Avenue, I struggle to cope with sensory overload: Diverse architecture invites appreciation, talented street performers compete for attention, taxi horns blare, and vehicle exhaust punctuates the aroma of ethnically diverse food. It takes a lot of mind energy for me to weed out the distracting noise of traffic and music. Just navigating the crowds on the city streets takes energy away from my creativity.

In contrast, when my choreographer friend from New York visited me, he couldn't handle the deafening silence of my rural home. His mind had adjusted to the hustle and bustle of big city life. Some people need this higher level of stimulation.

*At home, do you leave the TV on for background comfort?*

*Do your kids have ear buds stuck in their aural cavities?*

## 2. Cluttergories

Sensory overload leaves many people needing to escape the city for a tranquil mountaintop for inspiration.

We can create similar tranquility by turning off the noise or putting in sound-dampening earplugs, which Brenda does on airplanes and when sleeping in noisy cities.

While big city life has its advantages, including having everything close by and easily accessible, one disadvantage is our inability to be alone with our thoughts.

Sights and sounds aren't the only sensory clutter. You can experience overload inhaling too many aromas in a brief period.

Brenda relates: "During the rare times when my husband, David, and I shop for a new perfume or cologne, our noses lose their sensitivity after the third or fourth sample. We have to walk away for a while before returning to make a decision."

The same holds true for enjoying different tastes.

David and Brenda serve on their community's wine-tasting committee. Each year they select ten of the finest red and white wines, plus one dessert wine. Some evenings, they go overboard and taste too many wines. Toward the end of the evening, their pickled tongues are useless and their noses can't smell.

Even one's sense of touch can be overwhelmed.

Nothing feels more invigorating than a deep-tissue massage. Unless you overdo it—as Brenda did once while at a conference. After three consecutive days, any therapeutic benefits were replaced by pain.

Too much of anything sensual—sights, sounds, tastes, touches, and smells—will over-stimulate us and diminish our enjoyment.

Using the five cluttergories as a starting point, let's get our minds out of the clutter.

# Part Two:
# Does Stuff Matter?

Hell, yeah!
Especially when disaster
threatens everything
you own.

# 3. The Station Fire

An arsonist started the Station Fire[6] on August 26, 2009. It burned for almost two months until October 16, and consumed over 160,500 acres (250 square miles) of the Angeles National Forest in northeastern Los Angeles County. It damaged homes and businesses and took two lives. For two weeks, while the Station Fire gripped Brenda's community in a chokehold, she wrote the following:[7]

The Station Fire is only 42% contained as it continues moving east along the northeastern area of the Angeles National Forest toward our home. At our elevation—ranging from 4,000 to 5,000 feet—the air appears clean above the haze and dust in the valley below.

However, this week, the smoke is thick. My throat is burning, my sinuses are swelling, and my head is aching. David is at work while I work from home and monitor the situation.

I can't get any work done. I'm afraid. My brain needs oxygen.

Victimized by the whims of the ever-changing winds and flying embers, I'm reminded of the years David and I cared for my father. We were unprepared for the crisis of caregiving. My father was diagnosed with dementia and was getting worse by the week. Something had to be done.

Likewise, we are inadequately prepared to accept our fate as the fire moves closer.

Surprisingly, we have an Internet connection and phone service. We get updates from county and national websites on the direction, speed, and proximity of the fire. Google Earth images help us visualize where we are in relation to the neighboring mountainous terrain being swallowed by the fire.

We gain some comfort, being able to share telephone updates—even with members of our community who live along the ridge where the fire is climbing.

Early on, David and I decided which trips to town were absolutely necessary. We're scared and stressed. We know enough to conserve our energy. We agree that one of us must stay at home to notify the other in case the situation changes.

While we're both home, our cars—filled with a fraction of our possessions—are backed into the garage. We're ready to drive straight out at a moment's notice.

## 3. The Station Fire

The fire is moving closer. We have to evacuate. We are unprepared, urgently contemplating what really matters in life. Each of the three times we're asked to evacuate, we wonder: *What really matters when we're faced with losing everything?*

I revisit the question I asked many times while my father lived with Alzheimer's disease: *What really matters?*

LIFE. That my husband and I and our kitty cat are safe ... that our neighbors are also safe.

Saving our shelter. David has stretched hoses across our five acres ready to draw on 13,000 gallons of stored water. Despite that 4,800 personnel assigned to this record-breaking fire are doing all they can to protect us, the winds are unpredictable in our foothills, and all it takes is one fallen ember to ignite.

If we can't save our shelter, we'll at least save some of our possessions. But which ones? Overwhelmed by losing everything, I freeze. My mind goes blank. David's overwhelmed too and sighs, "Just leave it. It's too much." (I wonder if he's referring to all his toys in the garage!)

It's during urgent times like these when our possessions paralyze us. How do we gather our precious possessions when they're spread throughout our home?

The cars are packed—laptop, external backup drives, two changes of professional clothing, and casual clothes, are squeezed in among the cat supplies—litter box, carrier, toys, blanket, food, and medicine.

The phone rings. My neighbor, a forest ranger, calls to give me a status update. He volunteers that his wife is removing pictures from the walls. *Pictures! I completely forgot!* I run around to gather our family photos, videos, and even remove a handful of framed images off the walls ... I grab one copy of each of the books I've written and their foreign editions. Oh, and I need to pack the wooden spoon.

*Wait! Where's the wooden spoon?*

# 4. The Wooden Spoon

After Brenda's mother died in 1993, her father and her were reminiscing in the attic of his Wisconsin home of forty-plus years. When they opened the leather travel trunk her mother carried when she immigrated to America in 1949, they found a well-preserved cashmere sweater with mother-of-pearl buttons neatly folded among her mother's things.[8] Brenda shares this reflection:

My father urged, "Take it. It'll look good on you, Brenda."

I declined. "You know what I'd really like?"

"What?"

I unfolded my legs, got up.

"Where you going?" my father asked.

"To the kitchen," I said as I skipped down every other step of two staircases.

Curious, he skipped steps too and we jokingly elbowed each other as we tried to squeeze through the kitchen doorway at the same time. I stood in front of the original 1930's steel kitchen cabinets and pulled open the silverware drawer. I looked along the left side where the serving utensils were and reached in. My fingers fumbled about the utensils until I found the wooden spoon. My mother stirred whatever ingredients she had on hand into fragrant and tasty soups and stews with this spoon. As a child, I'd beg her for samples.

"That?" my father asked. "Why do you want that old thing? Here, take this one," he insisted, retrieving a newer spoon.

"No, I want *this* one," I said, clutching the old wooden spoon. "This is the one she'd threaten me with when I'd get into trouble!"

## Why Some Stuff Matters

Like my parents, I realize I hold onto *things*. The old wooden spoon matters. So does the cashmere sweater that I took during a later visit but have never worn. The old-fashioned food scale my parents used to weigh watermelons also matters, but I rarely use it now. I can't even tell you where it is. But I do display my mother's *tsera khordz* (embroidery).

## 4. The Wooden Spoon

It seems that having stuff is a part of our DNA. We are wired with a need for STUFF.

Even squirrels bury seeds and nuts in the late fall. During the winter, they feast on those stored seeds and nuts. But, we humans store more than enough to carry us through a season. Many of us suffer from "STUFFitis," the disease of having too much. Some of us have so much stuff we freeze with indecision while a fire or other disaster races toward our home. Instead of gathering what we treasure most, we do nothing because we can't find "the wooden spoon" in our lives.

One reason our stuff matters is it reminds us of the people who left an impression on us—like the wooden spoon serves as a reminder of my mother's cooking.

With both of my parents now gone, the wooden spoon takes me back to my youth. Forty years ago, those tantalizing aromas rising to my bedroom from the kitchen below, made my mouth water. I'd run down the stairs and beg Ma for samples of her unique blend of soups and stews. I can still taste her barley and oxtail stew with freshly sliced carrots, ripe tomatoes, zucchini, and verdolagas (purslane) gathered from her garden. (I've even managed to make it several times.) Those spoonfuls would tease my taste buds into wanting more. I'd beg, and sometimes she'd relent with the warning: If you keep eating now, you won't have room for dinner. Other times, when I'd pester

Ma too much, she'd stop stirring the soup, tap it on the edge of the pot to remove the drippings, and then shake it at me to shoo me away.

We need to ask ourselves, "Do I have so much stuff that if disaster threatened, I wouldn't know what really matters?"

Only you know what is important to you.

And yes, it can be difficult to decide what to keep and what to toss or donate. It isn't a question of needing it at this moment. Sentimentality often trumps practicality. Sometimes stuff matters, even if it is neatly stored *away* and out of mind.

# 5. A Man's ~~Home~~ Garage is His Castle

Eric believes a man's home is his castle, unless the man's wife says otherwise.

Men and women view things differently because men and women ... well, they're different! In the past, gender stereotypes dictated that a woman commanded the kitchen while the man hid in the garage. The family room was often up for grabs, depending on who got the TV remote first.

*What the heck does that have to do with clutter?* Plenty.

Fellow men, I ask you, what happened to the adage that *a man's home is his castle?* If we're lucky, we're left with the garage. The garage—our *man cave*—filled with our stuff: workbench, power tools, in-progress projects, and a fridge full of beer. AHHHH, now, that's dreaming . . . because the reality is different.

Eric shares his reality:

The workbench is mine, *supposedly*. It is a flat surface I keep clean. But the workbench is right next to the door leading into the house—a perfect spot to set stuff down *temporarily*. The problems start when things migrate *out of* the house and land on the workbench temporarily—such as a quick cleanup of clutter when unexpected guests arrive.

Eventually things pile up because the items on the workbench have been there *temporarily*, for months. *What the hell happened to my workbench?*

*And where do I put all the stuff in the garage that isn't even mine? Why do I need a box of Barbie dolls, VHS tapes, and collector thimbles?*

*Oh yeah*, I *don't!*

But, if I want to stay married, I've got to find a place for it in my castle, temporarily.

*Temporarily? That was five years ago!*

And now, the VHS tapes have a broken VCR to keep them company.

The trailer? Okay, I can't blame that on anyone but me. About fifteen years ago, I wanted my own landscaping business. I bought a 4 x 8 utility trailer. I even upgraded the trailer with a custom enclosure and toolbox. I never started the business. Ouch. But I've used the trailer at least seven times over the last eleven years, so it has clearly paid for itself. I had a "For Sale" sign on it for a few months, but no one could see it inside the garage facing the workbench.

My philosophy is: *I would rather have it and not need it, than need it and not have it.*

It's a good thing there is storage space under the workbench. You never know when you'll need that ten-gallon fish tank again or the red Radio Flyer wagon. The baby stroller next to it should come in handy as well. My girls are grown now and they may give us grandchildren. We have to be ready for these major life events. Besides, if I got rid of the stroller, the high chair would be lonely. What about the baby clothes stored in bins on the shelf? They never go out of style! The turkey deep fryer on the top shelf that I bought on clearance a dozen years ago will surely get used *this* Thanksgiving. I should probably open the box to see how it works.

That's perfect because the Christmas boxes are right next to the deep fryer, which will help me remember to use it this year. Just like the snow skis I haven't used since high school, next to the Christmas boxes, helped me remember to book the ski trip last winter. *Wait, we stayed home last winter.* Never mind. The point is I may need these things *some*day.

Back to the kitchen. The way we've run our home, the kitchen is my wife's domain, which she runs with an iron mitt. However, the counter next to the sink is a sore point for both of us. It's her kitchen, but I use it too. *Is it unreasonable to expect a towel to be within easy reach?* We keep the towel on the counter next to the sink, but it's often under the mail, a magazine, or grocery ads. Boy, there's nothing like the smell of soggy paper in the morning, from wet hands searching desperately for the kitchen towel.

At least the family room is mine, right now. I have the TV remote. *Why is it wet?*

# 6. Those Are MY Toys

Are memories for sale? Sort of ... if they're toys!

Kids want all kinds of toys. What is a parent to do? What's *in* this season may be *out* next year—going from must-have toy to useless clutter in no time flat.

When Eric was a kid, he loved science fiction. As an adult, he finally had the means (money) to buy the STAR TREK and STAR WARS toys he wanted. And he did.

Eric shares his philosophy:

Toys should be played with. Collectible toys should be displayed where you can see them and appreciate them. My collection is neither played with nor displayed—it is simply boxed. Not quite out of sight, and never completely out of mind. I walk by them daily, they are important to me.

**Why do I hold onto my toys?** I have considered selling them on eBay, and even catalogued everything to do just that. But I didn't.

*Why not?* I could not let go. It is not about the money because, frankly, they are not worth much. It's more about what's of value to me in this moment—money or memories? Does two to three hundred dollars from eBay matter? Yes, money matters; but it pales in comparison to the joy of handling the toys, which trigger emotions of joy and memories, both real and imagined.

How do I put a price tag on a memory? I can't. I don't want to let go of the emotional high I get when I hold them. The toys win hands down. Even though they are in the way, they matter to me.

If I part with them, a part of me is gone. Forever.

Are memories for sale? No.

So, my toys sit in boxes until I can let them go.

# 7. Stuff Matters, But . . .

Ever heard the saying, "Too much of a good thing is too much?" It applies to stuff.

Yeah, we all have stuff. But there's stuff and then there's STUFF.

The reasons we hold onto stuff are as diverse and unique as we are.

However, since this is *STUFFology 101* and not a post-graduate course, we've distilled the reasons into three basic categories: holding onto memories, haven't had time to go through it, and no reason at all. (We're serious about the last one.)

We hold onto our stuff, such as sentimental keepsakes, memorabilia, and collectibles to remind us of people and events in our lives. The physical items, like a toy or a wooden spoon, anchor us to memories we cherish.

But what happens to all that other stuff that we don't have time to go through, like that backlog of magazines?

What happens when there's no more room for stuff in the garage?

What happens when disaster strikes and there's so much stuff we freeze with indecision?

We hold onto stuff that quickly becomes clutter for no reason at all.

This is where the problem lies—when we get stuck for no reason. We stumble as we try to step over or move around the clutter. Seeing our stuff every day in the garage and in our home overwhelms our minds with mental clutter. We know we should clean up the piles and organize the clutter but we do nothing.

And our inaction is what allows the clutter to grow. Which feeds our stress level . . . which makes us withdraw and avoid the issue ... which feeds our stress level ... which makes us withdraw and ...

*ARRRRRRGGGHHHHHHHH! I want my life back!*

# Part Three:
# I Want My
# Life Back

Damn it!

# 8. Where Stuff Comes From

*Well, it didn't just show up one day! Did it?*

It starts innocently enough. We take that one piece of paper and set it aside to deal with tomorrow. The following day, while rushing to complete an urgent task, we place another piece of paper on top of the first one. On the weekend, when we plan to catch up, a family emergency prevents us from processing that small pile of stuff.

There's always tomorrow. But, two months later, we still need to process that pile.

Like anything else in life, there's so much going on; we procrastinate doing certain things. We put off cleaning the garage, going through the closet, or making a decision on what to keep. We all do it. And then we're left with clutter.

Then there are the moments when we get a burst of energy to clean, like when company is at the door.

What happens after you clean off the dining room or kitchen table? You make a promise that paperwork will not accumulate there again. If others live with you, they too may make the pledge. You enjoy eating at the table once more. No more shuffling of paper to make a space to eat dinner.

Then what happens?

Someone places a piece of paper on that clean table *temporarily*. But it's still there. Even you ignore it, as you place something else on the table *temporarily*. A piece of low-priority mail joins these items. Again, it's just there *temporarily*, to be looked at later. Soon, you're grabbing trays and sitting in front of the TV to eat dinner.

*What happened?*

There's a scientific explanation—Newton's Second Law of Motion (the Law of Universal Gravitation): mass attracts mass.

When masses of clutter collide, it's not a good thing. The stories in Part Three have us wondering why we hold onto those toxic memories of the past. Why do we have a pool table if we can't play? When our children grow up and leave home, what do we do with their stuff? What about all those magazines and emails?

## 8. Where Stuff Comes From

*How will we get through all this stuff?*

The next story is a poignant reminder of the clutter in our lives. If we're not careful to reclaim our own lives by taking care of our clutter, we can severely affect another family's life long after we're gone.

# 9. The Toy Gun That Killed

One summer, Brenda's twenty-year-old nephew, Chris, was working at a major thrift store when he picked up a toy gun and began playing with it.[9] He was a fun-loving kid who brought joy to others' lives. While joking with his assistant manager as she sat at her desk and worked, he picked up what he thought was a toy gun from one of the shelves behind her desk. He pulled the trigger. Chris collapsed.

Figuring he was up to his usual antics, she called his name; then nudged him.

He didn't move.

She nudged him again, pleading, "Chris, c'mon, knock it off."

After all, the last time he did something silly he fell off a skateboard while testing it in one of the store aisles. He broke his arm and needed a cast.

Chris remained unresponsive.

According to the police investigation, it was a real gun registered in 1920. It belonged to an elderly couple who had since died. Although we can't know for sure, it's likely that the family gathered bags and boxes of things to donate without taking the time to go through all their loved ones' possessions. Perhaps the owner or a family member placed the gun at the bottom of the box to keep it safe and away from guests, only to have forgotten about it for years. Then the family unknowingly donated it.

---

*When you clear out your family's belongings, be careful to go through everything before you donate to a charitable organization.*

---

The family would be horrified to learn a life was lost because a young man whose life was just beginning to unfold had played with their family's gun.

The police said later that guns are donated unintentionally from time to time and they are called to pick them up.

Unfortunately, in this instance, Brenda's fun-loving nephew got to it first.

This is why we urge you, please, Please, PLEASE look through your boxes and bags of belongings before donating them. You may save a life.

# 10. The Ghost of Opportunities Past

Eric has worked in sales since 1990—that's over two decades. He writes: I can't let go of certain items from my first sales job with a wholesale nursery. *Why?*

I was laid off just before Christmas in 2008. This was during the recession and jobs were hard to come by. So why am I still saving stuff from that nursery? Is the paperwork a reminder of something I once enjoyed? It's a mystery to me now why I would need items from the job that cast me off. For a period, I was bitter and depressed, having invested all that time working for the nursery while sacrificing family time.

This is a good example of physical clutter cohabiting with mental clutter. It reminds me of something I once enjoyed; then grew to hate after being dismissed.

There was a lot of stuff going on in my life at the time. My youngest daughter was playing soccer. I was taking a night class at the local college. My wife was working more hours at her job. I was involved with a network-marketing company and attending trade shows on the weekends. I joined Toastmasters to be a more effective communicator.

Why do I still have leftover products and materials from the network-marketing company stored *temporarily* under the air hockey table in my game room? Despite all my efforts and sticking to the plan, the money never matched the hype of the picture-perfect rich lifestyle. My BIG effort returned a small reward. I am now left with a loose end in my life—mental clutter that still lingers. If I ditch the physical clutter from this network-marketing company, I can move forward.

If I had only known then what I grew to learn recently: We do what we can with what we have with where we are in life.

The lesson is not to become embittered over things that might have been. Letting go of our physical clutter releases the emotional baggage embedded within—our mental clutter. Of course, this is easier *read* than done.

I failed at this, initially. The layoff was a wake-up call to reevaluate what was important to me. A long, slow, and painful process—mental clutter is a bitch.

## 10. The Ghost of Opportunities Past

Clutter is a crutch for remaining stuck in the past and feeling sorry for ourselves. We hold onto stuff that doesn't serve us now. We need to process and then let go of whatever is holding us back. By doing so, we can accept, learn, and forgive in order to move forward.

Otherwise, we'll hold onto stuff that pollutes our minds, bodies, and homes.

And that just plain stinks!

# II. POOP!

There are **P**iles **of O**verwhelming **P**aperwork (POOP[10]) everywhere.

It stinks.

"And I'm constipated," laments Brenda.

In the last decade, Brenda has experienced firsthand a Mt. Everest of information. There's likely more information created each *year* than there was from the dawn of time to the 1990s. Imagine that. And the Internet is primarily responsible.

Advances in communicating instantly through multiple channels flood us with a mountain of information well beyond the daily newspaper. Social media platforms like Facebook, Twitter, LinkedIn, and Google+ vie for our attention with up-to-the-second updates. Emails fill our inboxes while ezines compete for our attention. Of course, some websites capture our interest and take us along links of scenic trails to other websites until we've done nothing else for two hours except wander around the mountain of online information.

## II. POOP!

When you add books and magazines, a lot of information piles up quickly as it vies for our attention. Soon, we're gasping for air as we try to ascend the Mt. Everest of information.

If we skim through everything, we'll not have a moment to get our work done.

Yet, what do you do if you're like Brenda and need to read everything you own?

Brenda shares her philosophy on POOP:

I resist the idea of living life a mile wide and an inch deep. I'd rather live each inch of my life a mile deep. I want the whole story *and the backstory*. I want to know the story from different angles.

How can I achieve such depth of knowledge when there's so much to read?

I set aside time to get through piles of paperwork, but it's hard to make time during my increasingly busy life.

Right now, I'm drowning in too many piles of overwhelming paperwork.

POOP! How appropriate, when I consider how often I've muttered to myself, "I need to get rid of all this $h!t ... uhh, I mean STUFF!"

I get POOPed just thinking about it! Come to think of it, it's building up and I can't seem to let it go! I need a diuretic to get rid of constipation caused by too much POOP! (Uh-hmm, I mean, Piles of Overwhelming Paperwork.)

Judging from the many articles written about it, POOP is a widespread problem. Heck, there's even a word coined around this problem. Dr. Audri Lanford and her husband, Jim, coined the term *paperitis* "to describe all ... [the] paper clutter and information ... that feels SO overwhelming."[11]

I suffer from paperitis and it has led to a buildup of POOP in my life.

Paperwork has remained my constant companion since I was eight years old. At first, I saved pictures of puppies and kittens, then recipes. Later, I saved my schoolwork. I still have my college coursework and my handwritten lecture and book notes—from thirty-five years ago! *Back then, Pluto was still a planet and Uranus was pronounced Yer-anus.*

In total, I've been fighting POOP (or suffering from paperitis) for forty-six years. Boy, do I feel constipated!

*I want my life back.*

But how?

I can't just toss my paperwork, as my husband does when his piles grow too tall. I feel a need to review, read, or scan all the books, magazines, and other papers before I let them go.

I want to enjoy more space in my home, to feel the energy of an open ambiance.

In 2004, my husband and I created more space when we bought a bigger home.

## II. POOP!

The open space helps me feel lighter and enables me to embrace new things. Fewer things mean less to worry about and fewer piles to trip over.

But there are still stacks of boxes, books, and magazines in my home office. I want to be able to walk up to my window and look out without stubbing my toe on a box. Besides, I'm tired of stretching over piles to look outdoors at a deer or a fox foraging for food. I'd like to spend less time during the weekends going through my boxes of accumulated paperwork and more time with people.

There's so much stuff, I feel like I'm flitting from one thing to the next. Am I a butterfly in springtime or do I have attention deficit disorder?

I want more energy to reflect on what's happening in the world.

I want to buy new books instead of catching up with older books.

I want to feel lighter and more energized.

I want to punctuate my work with more play.

# 12. Why Can't I Play Pool?

Eric reminisces: "I always wanted a pool table," probably because I had one growing up. Nothing fancy, just the cool factor. Thirty years later, my family has a game room with a dartboard, air hockey table, ski ball, pinball machine (now broken), and a pool table. We even have the same lamp that hung over my parents' pool table. Truth be told, I never wanted that lamp. I wanted a Budweiser lamp!

"I have it all. Right? Not quite …

"The pool table provides a large flat surface I can use to sort things—mostly paperwork. For months, I've stored years of Toastmasters material on it. Until I decide what to keep, I will not be able to play pool on the pool table I wanted so badly.

## 12. Why Can't I Play Pool?

"Not fun.

"Recently, my wife, Susi, needed to practice for a pool tournament—a fundraiser for her Relay for Life cancer walk team. She and our daughter Maggie offered to help clear the pool table.

*"Always accept help when it's offered, especially for something you don't feel like doing!*

"Unfortunately, they don't know what to keep or toss. And I do not agree with 'when in doubt, throw it out,' because *I would rather have it and not need it than need it and not have it.* So, Susi and I removed the material off the pool table, carried it into our daughter Beth's room, and neatly stacked it in piles on the bed, on the floor, and on any other flat surface we could find. Problem solved! Sort of.

---

*I would rather have it and not need it than need it and not have it.*

---

"Now, what about the rest of the house?"

# 13. Whose House Is It Anyway?

If your child moved out of the house years ago, why do you still identify the room by his or her name? Why is it still "Jackie's bedroom?" She hasn't lived at home for eight years. When is she going to take her stuff out of *our* house? Most likely answer: never.

After your children move out, is it still their room?

In Eric's case, the answer is yes … and no.

Yes, because he wants his children to always have a place to call home.

No, because his house is not a storage unit for his adult children's stuff.

They are moving on with their lives. It's not the parents' responsibility to store their adult children's stuff indefinitely.

## 13. Whose House Is It Anyway?

But, that's exactly what happened to Eric.

*How does this become a problem?*

Do you want your legacy to be a house full of stuff? We doubt it.

Clutter and sentimentality are intertwined. One cannot move forward without letting go of the past, in both the figurative and literal senses.

Eric explains: "I am a sentimental guy, something I inherited from my mom. This is also why I have the same packrat tendencies as she does. Namely, I have clutter because of my attachment to things that hold memories for me.

"Sometimes I like to reminisce and hold onto the physical objects as a memory trigger. But how much stuff do I need in order to do this? Not much, really. Probably less than I have."

When is it too much? Maybe it's too much if you need to ask the question.

One solution is to have your children sort through their stuff with you. Build new memories while clearing the clutter. As with so many things in life, we have to let go of the old to make room for the new.

Then, we take a step toward getting our lives back.

# 14. I Want My Life Back!

When faced with a disaster, like the Station Fire, we don't want to freeze like a deer in the headlights on a country road. We'd like to prioritize our stuff so our valued possessions are easy to grab without worrying that we might leave something behind.

*How could Brenda not find the wooden spoon?*

We are dealing with too much stuff, if we:

- can't easily find what we are looking for. *Where are my keys? Where's that document?*
- wake up at night feeling the need to do something about our accumulated possessions.
- have so much stuff we no longer remember what we have.

- are so overwhelmed we're only skimming through life.
- can't park the car in the garage.
- can't let go of a favorite toy.

When we fail to manage the clutter, we get stressed. *What can we do?*

---

*Studies estimate that 1.5 million Americans have so much stuff they can't use their kitchens, bathrooms, or bedrooms in the way they are intended.*

---

All the things we *need to do* impair our ability to comprehend, much less retain, what we *actually do.* How often have you read an article, set the magazine down to do something else, and forgotten what you read? If you're like us, you'll read most of the magazine, feel good that you read all the way through, only so you can toss it or give it away. *Do you remember what you read? Did you take time to think about what you read?*

If it's not attention deficit disorder then it surely must be Alzheimer's because we're flitting like a butterfly from here to there then forgetting.

We want to stop flitting around. We want to live with more purpose—to reflect and to derive meaning from what we read.

Yet, to make sure our hard work helps us achieve what we deserve, we need to *know* what we want.

*What do we want?*

- We want to feel lighter, freer, and not tied down by so many things.
- We want to overcome the CHAOS in our lives—Can't Have Anybody Over Syndrome[12] without spending a day cleaning.
- Brenda wants to clear her office of the six boxes under the table, the three against the file cabinet, and the assorted piles of paper.
- Eric wants to play a game of pool.
- We want less to maintain and worry about so we are free to do what we want.
- We want to take a trip on the spur of the moment.
- We want to buy new books and read them soon after we buy them, instead of waiting to read them after we catch up with all of our other reading.

Bottom line? We want fewer things to worry about, to take care of, to dust, and to process.

We know we can't own happiness by accumulating possessions. After wanting something for so long and then acquiring it, what happens? We use it and enjoy it; then something new comes along. We stop noticing the old stuff while acquiring new stuff.

*At what price?*

Taking care of all this stuff costs time, money, thought, and space. As time marches on and life passes us by, we wonder what potential relationships we are missing while spending time with stuff.

Soon we pay the ultimate price: allowing clutter to control our lives. Instead of bringing us joy, our clutter compromises our concentration, creates a toxic environment, and increases our stress.

We try to ignore it. We close the door to the room filled with stuff. We escape to a mountaintop or a beach to rediscover our muse. We can't escape. Our stuff waits for us at home.

Wouldn't it be nice to have a pesticide for clutter? Yeah, we could kill stuff with STUFFicide.

That would be too easy. We'd never learn how to manage clutter. We'd be stuck in a never-ending spiral, dealing with clutter and needing STUFFicide. Who wants that?

We believe it is time to pay the price *now* so we can enjoy life later.

Join us, and *get your mind out of the clutter.*

# Part Four:

# Get Your Mind Out of the Clutter

Clear your stuff.
Clear your mind.

# 15. Define Your Clutter

*In what areas do you have too much stuff?*

Everyone defines clutter differently. Brenda learned this the hard way.

She writes: I invited several neighbors to tell me what they thought of the boxes I had tucked in a corner of my office. One neighbor, whose wife is a self-labeled packrat and who rarely invites anyone inside their home, kept looking around, waiting for me to show him the cluttered areas. He didn't view the fifteen boxes in my office as clutter.

More recently, after successfully taking small steps, eliminating five of those boxes, and eagerly seeking validation—I asked my British neighbor what she thought. Twenty years ago, she immigrated to the U.S. with all of her possessions in *one* suitcase. She regularly inventories the things she's accumulated in her home and donates what she no longer needs. She looked at me earnestly, wondering if I could handle her assessment.

When I assured her I wanted her *honest* opinion, she replied, "Oooh, Brenda. I would never let it get this far."

*WHAT?* So much for defining my own clutter and wanting validation!

At that moment, I thought *Wait, what do you mean? There are only ten boxes. You should have seen it when there were fifteen.* However, true to my word, I thanked her for the honesty. When she left, I looked at that corner of my office. Sure, there were books on those boxes, files, and magazines leaning against them, but at least I didn't accumulate more *boxes.*

The importance of defining your own clutter can't be overstated. Your perspective uniquely frames perception.

When we talk about clutter, we often picture physical clutter as Brenda relates below.

## PHYSICAL

I am reminded of a line I read in a book on feng shui years ago: *Nature abhors a vacuum.*

When you create an empty space by getting rid of old or unused belongings, the void or vacuum seems to invite new things.

When we were selling our home in the city to move to the rural home we're living in now, the Realtor had us remove half of our stuff so people could more easily picture their belongings in our home. The widow who bought it commented on the spaciousness of our home.

Once in our new home, I removed the clothes I wore in my twenties. I donated them to my friend who served on the children's hospital board for their fundraiser. Letting go of those quality-made tailored clothes created a vacuum with such a powerful force that soon my walk-in closet featured new clothes that actually fit. Plus, I felt better about walking into a more spacious closet.

That doesn't mean I got rid of *every*thing. Eric and I agree that the oft-cited rule to discard or give away things we haven't used in over a year is just plain rubbish.

The time-elapsed-since-last-use rule is just plain wrong!

Just because I haven't worn a piece of quality clothing for seventeen years doesn't mean it won't be useful someday. *I'm serious!*

In 1983, I spent a small fortune ($30) on a heavy, hand-knit, wool sweater at a clearance sale. I liked how warm it kept me during the cold Wisconsin winters. But the collar was too tight and choked me. I stopped wearing it until 2007, almost a quarter century! It took me that many years to figure out that a tailor could cut down from the neckline and sew in a six-inch zipper. Today, this sweater, which would cost about $200 if I could even find one, keeps me warm at night when car-camping in the Sierras.

On the other hand, I'm good about getting rid of things I know I won't need—such as old furniture, appliances, knickknacks, and more.

My problem lies with paper and book clutter.

My goal is to get rid of half of my library of books and materials. However, I have one borderline compulsive tendency: I need to read or review every book and piece of paper from my thirty-year career. A snail could win this race, as I've only processed five boxes in ten years.

---

*One in ten U.S. Households (10.8 million) rent a self-storage unit—a 65% increase since 1995 when only 6% rented one.*

Source: Self Storage Association 2012 Mid-year report

---

**Renting storage space should be a temporary solution.**

Sometimes circumstances require that we store our stuff—our home sells faster than the home we're buying is available or we're on an extended assignment overseas. Whatever the reason, storing things should be a *temporary* solution, not a *permanent* one.

Don't rent storage space in order to postpone making decisions about what you should get rid of now. *Do you still need your collection of pet rocks from the 70s?*

With time, we'll forget about what we've stored,

despite spending hundreds, if not thousands, of dollars a year in storage fees.

Physical clutter is only a fraction of the clutter we must manage. There are four other cluttergories: digital, mental, temporal, and sensual.

# DIGITAL

Accumulating too many files on our computers, smartphones, tablets, and other devices becomes digital clutter if we can't find what we need.

Brenda explains: There are 150,000 pictures, videos, books, and documents on my husband's and my desktop computer. I often wonder what to do with all that information.

On the other hand, my husband doesn't view digital files as clutter because the computer case that holds them remains the same size.

I disagree.

I would be buried in digital clutter if I didn't take time to review and consolidate my files regularly. This doesn't include the 1,000 or so emails I deal with each week. If I don't visit each of my email accounts daily, I will easily drown under the onslaught of emails.

On the other hand, my husband uses the search feature frequently to find what he squirreled away on the hard drive.

And this is important to know when dealing with our own and others' clutter—*each of us defines clutter differently.*

Clutter blocks our progress and inhibits our creativity, whether it's our clutter or someone else's.

Since I began using computers in the 1980s, through trial and error, I learned how important organizing my files was to my day-to-day functioning. Initially, there were hundreds of files. A decade later, there were several thousand. The decade after that there were 50,000 to 75,000, and now there are 150,000 files.

When a former neighbor passed away years after he had moved out of state, his son asked for certain photos I had taken years earlier. He wanted them for his father's funeral. Although I had emailed him the photos, he could not find where he stored them. Fortunately, because of the way I organize my computer files, I was able to locate them quickly. I keep our photos in four folders labeled by year—"Photos 2013–2014," "2011 and 2012 photos," "2008–2010 photos" and "2007 and earlier photos." I looked in the "neighbors" subfolder within the two earliest-dated folders and found the pictures. Within fifteen minutes, the son had a handful of photos in his inbox.

Are my digital files clutter?

Not if they remain organized and I can find what

I need without too much wasted time. Also, not if I have a use for them.

I didn't start this way. When we bought our first computer, my husband and I stored files and folders on the main drive of the computer. It was a mess! I wanted to organize them but hubby kept tossing items onto the hard drive. It was a constant struggle.

With a bit of magic, thanks to partitioning software, peace settled upon our home and computer after we created separate "David" and "Brenda" drives. This way, he continued "organizing" his files the way he wanted without encroaching on my system of organization.

Since those days, and now with gigabytes of memory instead of megabytes, we still maintain separate folders on the C drive for "Brenda," "David," "Photos 2013-2014," and so on. To keep our tens of thousands of photos organized, David downloads all photos in a temporary "Photos" folder on the desktop. I then file them away in the appropriate subfolders such as "caregivers," "neighbors," and "hikes."

However you manage it, get control of your digital life; otherwise, you'll grow overwhelmed quickly and create domestic digital warfare.

## MENTAL and TEMPORAL

Physical and digital clutter have ways of encroaching on our peace of mind.

When stuff overwhelms our space and we stay awake at night worrying about where something is, we've entered the zones of Mental and Temporal Clutter.

Our virtual (digital) activities online take time, including reading and responding to emails, staying active with friends on Facebook, and engaging with our Twitter followers, while being sure to Google+ and strengthen our connections on LinkedIn. When we can't relax because we have to be online constantly to keep up with all of the virtual demands on our time, we leave no time for reflection.

When boxes of physical clutter crowd our space and occupy our minds, they take valuable time (temporal clutter) away from more desirable pursuits.

Brenda writes about being preoccupied with unnecessary mental clutter:

I'd wake in the middle of the night and think about getting through my boxes. Even though they were neatly stacked along the wall and under a window, they occupied my mind. In the wee hours of the morning, I'd awake and go down to my office to reflect on my early years ... times in my life when I did things because I didn't know better. The papers stored inside those boxes uncovered painful memories. Sometimes, I let those early morning reflections ruin the rest of my day.

*How could I have not known?* I'd wonder as I reviewed a document. *All those days, months, and years I sacrificed quality of life to produce volumes of quality work. Time spent away from friends and family. No time for a vacation. No time to exercise.* I didn't take care of myself. *For what?*

**Why do I hold onto the physical remnants of these memories?**

The best I could figure, I held on for two reasons— to remember and for historical context.

By reflecting on what I defined as clutter, I was able to see more clearly the painful lessons I had not learned early on. Since I tend to forget negative experiences quickly, it's harder for me to learn their lessons.

For example, I learned in hindsight that I repeatedly gave people chances despite their excuses and continued lack of initiative. Their lack of commitment placed a greater burden on my life. We all know people who talk BIG then step back to let you do all the work. *No more.*

Only after I learned the lessons contained in the boxes, could I discard the source of those memories. There are more boxes and more lessons inside them … even as Eric and I write this book.

The second reason I keep what's in the boxes is for historical context. Each generation thinks they've come upon a new idea when most of what we treat as new is an old idea wrapped in new words.

> *Only after I learned the lessons contained in the boxes, could I discard the source of those memories.*

However you label it, define your clutter.

Is it physical, like my books and boxes?

Is it digital—you're overwhelmed by so many files you can't find what you're looking for when you need it?

Is it mental—your mind is filled with worry?

Is it temporal—your life is filled with so many detours you navigate through streets paved with unfinished projects?

Or is it sensual?

## SENSUAL

Do you strive for so many experiences that you no longer remember having them?

Touch, taste, smell, sound, and emotions can be toxic, numbing, and painful if we get too much.

Too much of a good thing stops being good when we can't take it anymore. Brenda loves a glass of fine red wine. Bring on the pinot noir, the merlot, a cabernet, Shiraz, or even Bordeaux. One evening, after sampling nineteen bottles during a wine-tasting committee meeting, too much of a good thing became toxic. On the way home, she thanked her husband for keeping a plastic trash bag and paper towels in his car. Nineteen one-ounce tastings were violently rejected by her body. *All that good wine ... wasted!*

Too much of a good thing creates overload and numbs your senses.

When we layer activity upon activity and need more than twenty-four hours a day to get it all done, we create cluttered lives and minds that won't calm down. We get plenty of exercise, though, jumping from one thing to the next, while losing focus quickly. We half-attentively talk with a family member while texting a reply to a colleague. To keep up, we need a digital calendar that notifies us of our next appointment with a sound. *We admit, without this, we'd be lost!* We remain on the move, never in the present, but always focused on our next activity.

It's no wonder our hyper-stimulated minds can't slow down enough to rest or sleep.

It's no wonder it takes us three days to start relaxing once we're on vacation. By the time we feel relaxed, it's time to return home.

**How do you get your mind out of the clutter?**

You begin by defining your clutter—what prevents you from doing what interests you *now?* Then, you start writing.

# 16. Write Down Your Thoughts

Our minds are constantly busy. Thoughts come in. Thoughts go out. Ideas meander or bolt in; then disappear. We spend time and energy trying to remember things. Writing down or recording what comes to your mind (on paper or on your computer, tablet, or smartphone calendar) insures you won't forget it. This simple act frees your mind from having to hold onto information. And, at the end of the day, you'll be able to lie in bed, relaxed, because you will have freed your mind of this mental clutter.

If ideas pop into your mind in the middle of the night and won't go away, grab that pen and notepad and write them down. Brenda says that doing so helps her get to sleep. She writes: I keep notecards and a penlight next to my bed; although, I only use them once or twice a year since I've made it a habit to write down my thoughts and ideas during the day.

As you incorporate this habit into your routine, you'll also need to look at your list or calendar throughout the day. Brenda adds: You don't want to be like my husband, who writes down his ideas but still forgets them because he doesn't remember to look regularly at his notes or calendar.

A strategy for those of you who are like Brenda's husband: use sticky notes and place them at eye level where you'll be sure to see them.

For example, write "Buy milk" on a sticky note and place it on the steering wheel. Be careful, though, with the notes you place on the steering wheel, especially if your car is parked in a public place. "Get cash" might invite unwelcome followers.

Defining your clutter and writing down your thoughts will help reduce the mental clutter that clouds your thinking and keeps you up at night.

*The next step?*

Focus on doing one thing.

# 17. Focus on Doing One Thing

**When you focus on the task in front of you, you will get through the clutter.**

If you're like Brenda, paper clutter occupies your thoughts. You wonder when you'll have the time to get through all of it; yet, you can't throw any of it away until you've looked through it once more.

Instead of getting caught up on reading everything, take Brenda's high school friend's advice—tear out the articles you plan to read now and toss the rest. Sure, someday you might need that article on spaceship etiquette during intergalactic travel, but more up-to-date articles will likely be available by the time you're ready for space travel.

Until then, take one magazine and skim through it. Go ahead. Try it. *Now.*

See?

How hard was that?

If you can't decide which articles to keep, tear out and toss the ones you've already read. At least your magazines will get thinner! If you're worried about not remembering something new, know that each newer piece of information will build on your past knowledge. Just as a 3-D printer builds layer upon layer until the entire object is formed, you too will build layer upon layer of knowledge.

"Okay," you say, "but I have a hundred magazines lying around. It'll take me longer than I have to live!"

Brenda agrees: I think of this all the time. For months, when the mail came, I'd place it on the lower-left corner of the kitchen counter. I figured when I saw it daily, I would go through it. That seemed logical, but in practice, as the pile grew, I became blind to it. I ignored it until company was at the door. Then I swiftly scooped up the pile of papers, envelopes, magazines, sales fliers, and tossed the bunch on a box in my office and closed the door.

Out of sight, out of mind.

After a few instances of swiftly scooping piles of paperwork, the foot-high pile weighed so much it punched through the top of the box onto the files stored inside.

I couldn't ignore it any longer. It festered and grew in my mind until I did something about it.

I pulled out the entire pile and sorted through it, tossed the expired sales fliers, and looked at the papers and magazines.

One or two nights a week, instead of mindlessly relaxing in front of the blur of news and entertainment on TV, I grabbed a few pieces off that pile and in an hour tossed or filed some, before returning what I didn't finish to the pile. It was frustrating at first. In fact, I gave up, initially. Then I tried again ... and failed.

After enough failures, I grabbed just one magazine.

I started small and focused on getting through just one magazine. The first took an hour and a half—it was interesting. I can't tell you what it was about, but I do remember being interested for about twenty-four hours in what took me ninety minutes to read. I remained confident that I was building layers of knowledge.

I ripped out the pages I read in the next magazine, filed some and tossed most. That took forty-five minutes.

Going through that pile felt like eternity; especially, as I grew overwhelmed by the other piles of magazines propped up alongside my boxes and on the bookshelves.

I stayed committed to the task. Eventually, I had whittled away at that one-foot pile until one day, I was surprised to see only a few inches remained—a sizable achievement.

I continued until only a handful of magazines remained.

Strengthened by my progress, I went upstairs and removed the seven-year-old pile of magazines on my nightstand—magazines that had languished there since 2004, the year we moved into the house we live in now.

Because I had to read everything once more before I could let it go, I started the process of nibbling away at the articles. I read about mini carrots. I thought they grew that way—not so! They are full-sized carrots cut into bits then smoothed out to look like mini carrots. The peelings are used for juice and animal feed. *See? Had I simply tossed those magazines, I would have never learned that!*

Over time, the cleared areas raised my confidence and my energy level. Soon, I looked through my clothes and got rid of any I wasn't likely to wear again. I donated unused office equipment that was taking up space and being used as an end table by our guests. I was able to reorganize my home office and make things more easily accessible. What I anticipated would take only two hours took the entire day, but I was invigorated by my newly organized office.

Over the last six years, I've been tackling my backlog of emails. Using a similar technique and the maxim *small steps repeated equal miles completed,* I've managed to reduce thousands of emails to hundreds. It's an ongoing process that I am committed to learn from rather than hitting the "delete" key repeatedly. I am learning how to manage a hundred emails to eight email addresses daily to prevent digital clutter from accumulating again.

Start small and focus on one area at a time. You won't feel as overwhelmed when you limit yourself. Plus the energy you feel from finishing one area will drive you to the next.

It does not need to take a lot of time; the goal is simply to finish one section, because success breeds success.

### What if stuff remains?

*So what?*

Remember, *done* is better than *perfect.* It's okay as long as it is organized and accessible.

Only you know what you need to keep. Keep what is important to you. One size does not fit all.

## 17. Focus on Doing One Thing

Define the clutter in *your* life and focus on one task. If you commit to doing this even one hour a week; after fifty-two weeks—just one year during your life—you'll be surprised at how much clutter will disappear. Take *before*-and-*after* photos.

Don't give up. After only three months, you will feel a lot lighter, more energized, and confident.

You deserve to *get your mind out of the clutter.*

# 18. Dedicate a Workspace

*Where do you put the day's mail? Does it go on the kitchen counter or on the dining room table?*

*Do you have to clear a space at the table before sitting down to eat? Or do you grab a tray and sit in front of the TV?*

When Brenda gives speeches about managing clutter, she suggests to her audiences that people tilt all of the horizontal surfaces in their homes to prevent the accumulation of POOP (Piles of Overwhelming Paperwork). This usually brings laughter.

Seriously though, it is important to dedicate a space for your mail.

To avoid eating dinner on trays while watching TV, Brenda and her husband agreed to place a small four-shelf bookcase near the living room and stairs since they pass this area coming and going multiple times a day.

## 18. Dedicate a Workspace

Brenda writes: When David comes home with the mail, he sorts it and places the appropriate pieces on his and my shelves. Sometimes he places the mail on another horizontal surface—the piano or on the back of the sectional couch. I remind him, nicely, to sort it and place it on his or my shelf. He mutters something about having his hands full or being in a hurry, but returns to finish the job.

Before we set up this and the following system, Brenda explains, the bills would be buried with other paperwork and we wouldn't notice until the next month's bill contained a late fee. *OUCH*. After several instances of neglecting to pay our bills on time, we set up a system that works. David places all of the bills in a dedicated slot of the vertical tray on my desk. Since he chose this space, he's been great about making sure our bills are paid on time.

Brenda adds that none of the mail makes it into the kitchen. The kitchen table has been completely free of stuff for nearly two years, and we've fallen into a nice clutter-free routine. It's comforting to be able to sit down and eat at the table when we want. And when there's a knock at the door, we can welcome guests without having to scramble to set aside piles of paperwork.

As Brenda explains, it takes consistent effort. In the evening, if we're not too mentally exhausted, we'll turn off the TV after an hour or so and whittle away at what's accumulated on each of our shelves. We'll take an item that we want to read for an hour. What we don't finish, we'll return to the shelf.

It is liberating and even uplifting when the coffee table, sectional, kitchen table, and counter remain clear.

The key is to find a dedicated space you feel comfortable using and then keeping up the practice. No exceptions.

*Why?*

Because one piece of paper will attract another and another (remember the Law of Universal Gravitation: mass attracts mass)—and soon you'll be wondering why there's no place to eat at the table.

## Dedicate a Workspace

While working on a project, most of us will make a mess, which is why having a dedicated workspace is important. The size of your project will determine the space you need—a desktop file holder, a tabletop, a bookshelf, a box, or an empty drawer.

Dedicating a workspace will keep you organized, make for less clutter elsewhere, and ensure you don't waste time looking for things.

Is your work area clear of distracting items? Are the items you routinely use within easy reach?

Brenda says, "It surprises me how often I've pushed things to the side to deal with later. As they take up

## 18. Dedicate a Workspace

valuable space nearby, I have to resort to circus-style contortionism to get to the things I need on a regular basis. *Does this make any sense?* I've been a working contortionist for a long time. It's likely you have too.

"One year, I realized I could move the things I didn't use as often to a distant spot. Some stuff went into the back of a lower file drawer, the top shelf of my floor-to-ceiling built-in bookcases, and on top of the boxes in my home office. Removing things I didn't use cleared up space to access easily the things I needed more often.

"I didn't expect what happened next. Making just one adjustment—to keep frequently used items easily accessible—reduced much of my work-related stress."

If you're reading this at your workspace, stop a moment and look around. What can you move out of the way to reserve easy-to-access space for something you use more often?

*Stop reading and look around, now. Remove one thing. See? How did that feel?*

---

*Dedicating a workspace will keep you organized, make for less clutter elsewhere, and ensure you don't waste time looking for things.*

---

"When I'm preparing a speech," explains Brenda, "I stay better organized when I keep my notes and reference materials on a small worktable at one end of my office. If I'm traveling for a speaking engagement, I also place my satchel on this table. As I think of things I'll need, I pack them in the bag. By the time I'm ready to leave, everything is in one spot and ready to go.

"Then, when I return from the presentation, I unpack my satchel and put the materials where I can find them."

By dedicating a workspace for each of your projects and incoming mail, you will be able to focus more easily and feel less overwhelmed by your stuff. As you get better at managing the stuff in your life, you will refine the methods and keep your mind out of the clutter.

# 19. Repeat Small Steps

Small steps repeated equal miles completed. *A journey of a thousand miles begins with a single step.*

And then another step.

And another.

Brenda illustrates with this example: While training for a marathon, I ran down hills backward to reduce the stress on my knees. I don't recommend this for obvious reasons, but I was always amazed at how much terrain I had covered when I looked at a particularly long stretch of road or trail in front of me.

The same holds true for clutter. Take a photo of a cluttered area; then take small steps consistently to get rid of your clutter. After a month or two, look at the original photo. You will be amazed at how much *ground* you *un*covered.

Taking small steps regularly will clear your space exponentially.

The same holds true with digital clutter.

Brenda tells of the time when her husband, David, challenged her to stay away from the computer while they were on vacation:

I agreed. After all, I thought, I'm on vacation! I didn't look at another email. (This was before smartphones and tablets.)

When I came home and turned on the computer, 1,300 emails vied for my attention across my accounts. It took me six weeks to catch up with the backlog while cursing my husband's challenge.

After spending thousands of hours over the years, I've managed to pare thousands of backlogged emails down to hundreds.

Today, I try to keep each of my top-level accounts down to a handful of emails. It's almost impossible, like losing the last five pounds on a weight-loss program. I'm also working on reducing the project-specific subfolders I've created in each of these accounts by 75%.

What works best for me is to wake up before dawn on the weekends. I get a lot accomplished before David wakes and we eat breakfast together. Devoting several hours each day (weekdays too) is quite an effort, but reducing the backlog of emails while keeping the number of new ones under control brings me peace of mind. I can't simply say, "I'll deal with this *later*," because *later* comes with a bunch more emails. To be a responsible professional, I respond promptly.

## 19. Repeat Small Steps

On the other hand, David likes to work late into the night and use the "delete" key. He explains that if the emails are important enough, the people who sent them would follow-up or call him.

We disagree on this point because I think he places the burden on the sender. Instead of playing email volleyball, David's method forces the sender to run to the other side of the net to serve the ball again—frustratingly exhausting for the other person.

Then I remind myself of theologian Reinhold Niebuhr's Serenity Prayer adapted for use by Alcoholics Anonymous:

*God, grant me the serenity to accept the things I cannot change,*

*The courage to change the things I can,*

*And wisdom to know the difference.*

Digital clutter is not limited to emails. It includes files and documents we save on our computers and in the cloud. Digital clutter takes far less physical space—but don't let that fool you. It still takes a long time to process files on a computer. I have files created in a defunct version of PageMaker that are years old. Why do I hold onto them? Because I still want to review them. *Someday* I'll convert them into PDF documents.

Some people argue that we should digitize all our files to save space. Others believe that the cloud is the answer.

We disagree, partially. Always have a backup system in case the impossible happens when an online site's databank goes down and you lose all your data.

*Too big to fail?* Remember when a few large financial institutions went down? So too could the cloud pour forth your data in a rapidly evaporating rain shower.

It can even happen with your hard drive. Have you ever experienced a hard drive failure? If you answered yes, you know what that feels like. It's happened to Eric and me several times and we've learned to back up our data onto an external drive regularly.

To avoid the pain that comes with the potential loss of data, save hard copies of treasured documents and photos. Just be selective in what you hold onto in order to avoid accumulating clutter.

Physical clutter requires similar baby steps like those Brenda took when she decided to process the fifteen boxes stacked in her home office. She writes: I set aside several hours one weekend a month for the task. After years of sustained and diligent effort, including sessions when I took tiny steps (reviewing one sheet of paper, two magazine articles, and an eight-page newsletter), I noticed a big difference. What a surprise to see only a dozen boxes remaining.

*See? Small steps repeated led to three boxes being eliminated.*

## 19. Repeat Small Steps

Try as I might, I couldn't bring myself to reduce further the dozen boxes that remained. For several years, I was lucky to make just one inch of progress. However, just as POOP has the potential to constipate, I felt miserable and had to do something about those boxes or else face the consequences.

Diligent small steps repeated during ongoing monthly sessions . . . *finally!* What a joy to see two more boxes disappear!

The time I invested in this process guarantees I will never regain this level of paperwork. *It's just too painful!*

But life is not linear. Sometimes we take a step back before moving forward. In ten years, I processed five boxes. However, paperwork, magazines, and books kept coming in; so these days, I take small steps each *week* instead of several hours a month. This doesn't work perfectly though. When I'm busy working on a major project with a deadline looming, I stack newsletters, magazines, and books on top and alongside the ten remaining boxes. I should probably put them in another box, but that would be disheartening after the progress I made in ten years.

I realize this is an *illusion* of progress. This illusion works for *me*.

The important point is we do whatever it takes to make *lasting* progress. In other words, sometimes we need to do what it takes to feel we are getting our minds out of the clutter.

There are no shortcuts for breaking old habits.

Managing clutter is like dieting. You can't fast for a week, because you'll be miserable and then gorge the next week. You have to take it a little at a time and learn any lessons along the way. Sometimes, you might gain a couple pounds, despite exercising and limiting how much you eat. Likewise, you might accumulate a stack of mail or paperwork while you concentrate on clearing other areas.

Managing clutter is the sum of small steps repeated until miles are completed.

Just as I had to condition my muscles, heart, and lungs before I walked out the door in 2011 to run a full marathon, getting rid of clutter entails similar conditioning. We train ourselves to repeat small steps until one day we look at the *before* photos and celebrate all the space we've created.

Inch by inch we accumulate possessions. And inch by inch, we need to let go for lasting change.

Consider the old health maxim—an apple a day keeps the doctor away. Can you imagine making up for two weeks of neglect by eating fourteen apples in one weekend? The same applies to getting rid of clutter.

## 19. Repeat Small Steps

You can't get rid of all your clutter in one weekend. Research and common sense show that a series of small steps are more achievable than one big step, which can be overwhelming and intimidating.

When is the best time to start? *NOW!*

# 20. Do It NOW!

Unless you want others going through your stuff, you'd better start getting your mind out of the clutter NOW.

*You'd hate to have people find something that you weren't ready to share, right?*

*Can you imagine donating an item that would take a life?*

"Okay. Okay," you say. "Where do I begin?"

Any place you're willing to start, right *now*.

Start with the messy cabinet in the bathroom or the workbench in the garage. Brenda started cleaning closets because they were where her husband tossed everything when guests arrived.

Remove items you've stopped noticing while dusting shelves. *Why keep dusting stuff that no longer holds your interest?*

Small steps lead to mini successes. As you grow confident, you will be able to take bigger steps.

## Procrastinating

The work that needs doing has a way of growing in our minds. Soon, the thought of reading the mail or clearing the kitchen table grows to the size of Mt. Everest. We feel overwhelmed.

This is the mental clutter that clogs our minds. When we finally decide to do what needs doing; surprisingly, it goes quickly. We're left scratching our heads wondering why we let it fill our minds with worry.

The bonus is the relief and lightness we feel after completing just one task.

But there's a dark side that threatens our progress: TV.

## Turn Off the TV

We underestimate the time we spend in front of the television. Brenda called her satellite TV provider to suspend service. At first, she found it was difficult because she missed the shows she and her husband were used to watching. Soon she and David filled their evenings with reading or watching old VHS tapes (before discarding them).

Try it. You'll be surprised how much time this frees up each day for letting go of things, spending time with people, and even talking with each other.

# Life Passes By

There might be times when you feel life is passing you by while you're reducing clutter. Whether you focus and take one small step at a time depends on your definition of clutter and what you want to achieve. Life moves forward and so do we—sometimes slowly, other times too quickly. What will make you feel better? Taking time to get through your emails? Clearing a kitchen drawer of never-used utensils? Sorting through clothes from leaner times? Reading a magazine? Or turning your back on clutter for a fun weekend with your friends? Only *you* can decide.

# Wasted Time

Researchers who study productivity claim that we spend an estimated two weeks each year looking for something. This is both frustrating and wasteful. Consider the following two points of view.

First, let's say your employer gives you two weeks of vacation a year. Are you willing to give back those two weeks because you wasted that time looking for things during the year? Imagine not having a vacation or being able to spend time with friends and family because you had to look for things. *Remember, when you said you'd put it away later?*

Second, would you pay a vendor or contractor one billable hour each day to look for misplaced items?

*We wouldn't!*

Consider these two perspectives the next time you set something aside to put away *later.*

## Do One Thing Now

Finishing one thing now is better than trying to do two things *later.* Remember, take one small step at a time; otherwise, you'll be climbing an overwhelming pile of clutter.

If you're struggling with this concept, go back and review the chapter titled "Focus on Doing One Thing."

Notice how much better you feel when you do what needs doing *now?* You will expend less mental energy on distraction and worry, while having more time and energy to do what you want.

Do it now because everything that comes in (input) must be processed (throughput) in order to find a way out (output).

# 21. Input, Throughput, Output

Managing clutter involves a simple formula: what comes in is processed, then something needs to go out, *or else*. If you put food in your mouth (input), your stomach and intestines will process or digest the nutrients (throughput), then expel the waste from your body (output). Imagine what would happen if you didn't let go of this waste. Soon enough, you'd be constipated. If you still refused to let go, the toxins would build up and you could die.

Nature's process is the key to get our minds out of the clutter.

When you bring something into your home—a magazine, a collector's item, an article of clothing, or a tool—let go of something to prevent potential toxic buildup of clutter.

## 21. Input, Throughput, Output

Brenda confesses her bout with temptation: When my husband comes home and excitedly tells me his friend will give him a $1,000 drafting table for free, I ask David what he plans to get rid of before bringing it home. (His friend is getting married and purging in order to combine two households.) Even I'm tempted by the offer. *A $1,000 adjustable-height-tilting drafting table? That would be cool to have. Where would we put it?* I'm not ready to let go of my new worktable and the boxes underneath. As David thinks about it too, he isn't ready to let go of his tools or the desk in the garage to clear enough space for a drafting table.

---

*Take in what you need. Use it. Then let it go.*

---

## Reduce Input

Reduce your input so you have less to worry about. It's harder to get rid of something once you own it. It's easier to not bring it home in the first place. You'll have fewer things to clean, maintain, and organize. You'll also spend fewer hours trying to get rid of stuff.

Before you buy that thing *ya' just gotta have,* THINK. What are you willing to get rid of first? Do you really need it? Can you wait a week before you buy it? Your answers to these questions will help prevent *premature shopulation.*

Whenever you go shopping, create a list and try to stick as close to it as possible. There's a science to product positioning in store aisles and most of us have not been inoculated to overcome temptation.

One way to reduce impulse buying is to add items to your shopping list as you run low on supplies. Keep the list in the same place—on the refrigerator, on the edge of the kitchen counter, or in another easily accessible spot.

Brenda has kept a weekly shopping list for decades. She writes: These days, I transfer the list to my online calendar then sync it to my smartphone, which I refer to while shopping. Today's smart fridges even include an electronic display of your shopping list that you can sync with your smartphone.

Still, because we have not been inoculated, we'll give into temptation and our twenty-item list will expand to twenty-three. Brenda adds: We discuss and agree before buying those extra items; otherwise, we wait a week or two to decide if one or both of us really needs that item. That's how an electronic food scale finally found a home on the counter next to the microwave. Even after waiting a week, I *needed* it. And the $5-off coupon helped.

By keeping a list and postponing impulse purchases, we avoid waste.

Otherwise, one item here, another item there, and soon the input of stuff grows toxic.

*Subscriptions are especially insidious.*

Subscriptions trickle in harmlessly—one magazine, book, or DVD each month. Even wine, beer, and fruit subscriptions can get out of hand quickly once you're no longer in the mood for something. So too, collector plates, trinkets, and more.

When you get behind using everything that comes in, you find piles that reproduce like rabbits. Soon you're tripping over stuff trying to get to the things you need. Your subscriptions no longer provide a FUN diversion. Instead, they become toxic.

If you're trying to clear the clutter in your life, don't subscribe to anything beyond the magazines that come with your professional affiliations.

---

*Don't subscribe to anything—videos, music, newsletters, magazines, or collectibles, until you've successfully managed the clutter in your life.*

---

After seeing the cumulative effect of magazines piling up on our shelves, boxes, and countertops over the years, we gradually let go and stopped the inflow by not renewing our subscriptions.

As you take steps to manage clutter, you'll create space in your life to discover and enjoy new interests.

*Think about how you want to spend your time before you subscribe to anything.*

If you must buy a magazine, buy a single issue. Yes, it costs a fortune for a single issue compared to the per-issue price of a yearly subscription. However, consider the price you pay in time and worry while holding onto and trying to read all of those back issues.

By reducing the input—the most important stage in this cycle—you will make progress in clearing your clutter.

# Incremental Throughput

Turn off the TV one day a week and spend an hour to digest meaningful tidbits of information. Imagine how good you'll feel when you get to read a *current* magazine. With less mental clutter clouding your thoughts, you'll be able to apply what you learn immediately.

It's this gentle process of digesting without a looming backlog of information that prevents indigestion and constipation.

When you get up to take a change-of-pace break, remember to pick up something and return it to its place. David used to complain, "How come I always have to clean up?"

I'd remind him, "Because you rarely pick up after yourself. Each time I get up, I put something away."

Use these one-hour periods to process your junk drawer or that small pile of mail before it reproduces. Decide to let go of that small kitchen appliance you haven't used since you moved a dozen years ago, or that power tool with the frayed electrical cord.

While Eric and I write this book, we're focused on the latest information on clutter, writing, and marketing. Magazines, books, and articles fill my worktable and the *STUFFology 101* folder on my computer. Once we're finished digesting the information (throughput), we'll give most of it away.

All too often, instead of OHIO—Only Handle It Once, we've been guilty of OHIT—Oops, Handled It Twice. If you're like us, remember that throughput is a process. We keep applying the steps to get our minds out of the clutter. Over time, we become more efficient at digesting our clutter.

# Output—Let It Go

After you digest your input, let it go. Sometimes what no longer serves our needs can help others. For example, tear out then toss or give away the magazine articles you've read. When you do this one article at a time, it's easier to let go. When I decide to share an article with a person, I set it aside with a note at the top to that person. This way, when I see the article later, I won't need to recall what to do with it.

Do you have an item of clothing that you won't wear? Let it go. Do this with just one item. Do the same with that old VHS tape. Watch it if you must; then let it go, along with that music cassette.

Stopping Nature's process by taking in and not letting go creates bloat, decay, and constipation. Nature is about flow. If we hold on too long we get stuck.

Instead, we need to let Nature take her course. We take in what we truly need—what serves us *now*. We benefit from it, then let it go after it no longer serves us.

Over time, we'll suffer less from the toxicity of clutter constipation. We'll feel lighter and free to pursue what we deserve in life.

# 22. Two Magic Questions

We conclude this section by asking two magic questions. Your answers will move you closer to getting your mind out of the clutter.

After following the steps outlined in chapters 15 through 20, we no longer contort like circus performers to reach something we use regularly. We don't lose an hour a day looking for something. We don't freeze in our tracks because we can't find that sentimental treasure in an emergency. We don't feel helpless now that our space is clear of others' clutter.

Remember it is much harder to get rid of something than it is to acquire it. In "The Endowment Effect,"[13] Professor Tom Stafford of the University of Sheffield, explains why we value something more when we possess it. "The Endowment Effect" powerfully influences how we manage clutter. Because we have a tendency to hold on to what we have, we must ask the first magic question to overcome the force of ownership.

### MAGIC QUESTION #1: If I lost this item in a disaster, would I take the time to replace it?

*If the suit I haven't worn for thirty years was destroyed in a flood, would I go out and replace it?*

*If my Lionel train collection was destroyed in a fire, would I replace it?*

What if everything you treasured was driven out to sea during a tsunami or turned into ash during a fire? Which items would you try to replace?

Oftentimes there are things occupying space in our homes that we don't even remember owning.

"When I was a little girl," Brenda reminisces, "my mother asked me to reach into a kitchen drawer that didn't open all the way because it was blocked by the refrigerator. I reached in the back of the drawer and pulled out old metal Kroger-brand spice containers. Turning them upside down, I was surprised to see a blue ink-stamped price of 29 cents. My mother looked equally surprised, not by the price, rather by the spices. How strange that she didn't remember having those spices, I thought. Even now, I feel mixed emotions when I come across something I didn't know I had. Today, I will use it, display it, or get rid of it."

The second magic question, which requires more imagination, is:

**MAGIC QUESTION #2: What would the area you're focusing on look, feel, smell, or sound like if you cleared out the clutter?**

Your answers to this question will take time to imagine because vivid detail is a powerful motivator to get moving.

Hint: It's easier to answer if you focus on one small area at a time.

Brenda's experience racing against a former race-car driver illustrates the fear we feel while embarking on the road of getting rid of our stuff.

Brenda writes: On straight stretches of road, my newer and more powerful car helped me beat the race-car driver. Yet, each time I came out of a turn, he was well ahead of me. I asked him how this happened.

"Instead of trying to adjust your steering while going into the turn, Brenda, look ahead a little ways," he advised. "Your brain will tell your hands what to do automatically."

*What? If I don't focus on where I'm driving, I might crash!*

I trusted him enough to have him guide me, as I looked farther ahead with each turn. I enjoyed the ease with which my hands turned the wheel to where my eyes focused *ahead*. With each success in easily making the turn, I had less fear that I might lose control of where I was driving. *What a powerful technique!* Eventually, I gained the confidence to try it without him guiding me from the passenger seat. Miraculously, it worked!

Just as I need to look ahead while making a turn, I need to visualize the look, feel, and smell of an area with less stuff. This sends a signal to get my mind out of the clutter.

As I imagine one less box in my office, and no more newsletters, books, and magazines piled on top, I breathe more deeply. Visualizing the open space gives me confidence to take more steps to clear the clutter.

You too will feel the power inherent in visualizing and be amazed by the magical ease with which you'll clear your clutter.

Think about it …

- What is it worth to have less stress in your life?
- Do you wish you had time to do more of the things you'd like to do?
- Would it be worth going through these steps in order to enjoy life and feel happier?

## 22. Two Magic Questions

- What is it worth to unveil unexpected gifts as you get your mind out of the clutter?
- Is the short-term pain of reducing your clutter worth the long-term gain of getting more of what you deserve in life?

If you've been saying yes, Yes, YES, then read Part Five to find out what's in it for you.

# Part Five:
# WIIFM?

What's in it for me?

# 23. What's In It For Me?

A lot!

The benefits of getting your mind out of the clutter are greater than your investment in taking the steps in Part Four. Once you get rid of the stuff in your life on a regular basis, you will feel less discomfort and anxiety.

When you focus on and accomplish one thing, you will gain enough momentum to repeat small steps until you get through the areas that clutter your life.

You know this. We know this. However, we slip into old habits until something happens that leaves a memorable mark on our lives. For us it was caring for our aging parents. *What do we do with all their stuff?*

After applying the steps in Part Four, you will find that:

1. Your focus and comprehension have improved. After reading something, you'll actually remember. (Now, read that again.)

2. You'll have fewer things to move, store, lose, dust, or clean.

3. You can open the door for an unexpected guest and welcome him/her in without first needing to clean.

4. Your digital files will be organized and more easily accessible.

5. You will spend more time with people instead of things.

In addition to these benefits, you will encounter unexpected gifts—serendipitous opportunities and treasures. Who can anticipate such things as a financial windfall or a simple turkey deep fryer that brings families and friends together for the holidays? You can hope for these, but the unexpected gifts that come your way will be unique to you and your situation.

Finally, by helping others with the BONUS *STUFFologist's Guide,* you'll learn more about how to manage your own clutter.

# 24. The U.S. Savings Bonds Windfall

During the 1950s, earning $100-plus a week, Brenda's father withdrew $10 from every paycheck to buy U.S. Savings Bonds.[14]

In 1996, when her father was diagnosed with dementia, Brenda and her husband, David, returned to her childhood home in Milwaukee, where her father had lived for forty-five years. Brenda shares her story:

We tried to help my father organize his paper-work, but everything was a mess and David and I had to go through it all. (I inherited this quality.) We meticulously went through each file and pile. It was nearly impossible to determine what was important and what was not. We had to leaf through every piece of paper one page at a time, being careful not to overlook something—like a $1,000 U.S. Savings Bond tucked between two sheets of scrap paper or hiding in a one-and-a-half foot pile of newspapers. We found important documents, cash, and bonds. It was an overwhelming task that soon left us exhausted.

After lunch one day, I returned to the sunroom. I watched my father hunched over paperwork at his desk. Five arched windows lined three brick walls. Once framed by silk-lined drapes tied back to let the sun in, these *same* drapes, now rotted from fifty years of sun damage, were closed. A single light bulb on my father's desk illuminated one corner of this otherwise dark room.

I walked closer to look over his shoulder. He was organizing his bills. I sat in a chair by a bookshelf in the living room, only a few feet away from where he was working. Soon, I grew bored and turned my attention to the books in one of the built-in oak bookshelves along the wall. Some were my father's German-language books from his bachelor years; others were reference books he used for his work as a machinist. Two hardcover books covered with brown paper bags grabbed my attention. I tried to decipher the rubber-stamped letters on their spines. Reaching out, I pulled one off the bookshelf. A little package fell on the floor. After looking quickly at the book, an engineering manual of interest to my father, brother, or husband, I placed it back and reached down for the package.

## 24. The U.S. Savings Bonds Windfall

Three dry rubber bands bound an eight-and-a-half by three-and-a-half-inch packet. I scraped off the rubber bands and unfolded a letter-sized sheet protecting a stack of cards. When I turned them over to look at the front side, "1,000" caught my eye on the upper left and right sides. I looked at the card more carefully and read "Series E." It dawned on me—it was a thousand dollar U.S. Savings Bond! I lifted a corner of the first bond to look at the second card and saw the same writing. I lifted the second bond and saw yet another 1,000. I fanned them out like a deck of playing cards and counted, four thousand, five thousand, six . . . fifteen thousand . . . twenty thousand . . . twenty-five thousand . . .twenty-eight thousand dollars in U.S. Savings Bonds. My heart fluttered!

"Look what I found!"

Without even looking up, my father extended his hand and said, "Oh, give it to me. I'll look at it later."

I wrapped the paper around the bonds then stood up to hand the bundle to him.

He tossed the loosely wrapped stack of bonds on the upper right corner of his desk and then immediately placed the bill he was looking at on top.

I sat down again and then recalled David's experience helping my father who often set aside bills and other important documents to look at *later*, until he could no longer find them.

I had to get the savings bonds. I rose from the chair and approached my father's desk. As I reached to grab the bonds, he looked at me and asked, "What are you doing?" I pulled out the stack and showed him one of the bonds.

Still showing no interest, he placed the bundle in the drawer. "I'll look at it later."

*I had to get those bonds.*

A while later, David came into the sunroom to see what we were doing. I told him we needed to think about what we were going to eat for dinner.

He exclaimed, "We just ate!"

I emphasized, "But we need to plan what we want to make for *dinner!*" and motioned with my head toward the kitchen. He got my hint and we went into the kitchen. Excitedly, I told him about the bonds. We worked up a plan to retrieve them.

Returning to the sunroom, David distracted my father with questions about the papers on his bed, which was also in the sunroom. He swiveled around to move his chair toward the bed. With my father's back to his desk, I swiftly retrieved the bonds and walked back to the kitchen. This was a major risk. I considered what I had just done. *I was no better than a thief!* Trembling, I fanned through them; many were thirty years old.

## 24. The U.S. Savings Bonds Windfall

David and I estimated these bonds to be worth about four times their face value. I struggled to remain calm. My father had over $100,000 worth of savings bonds!

Unexpected gifts are not always so large. Sometimes, it's a simple gift at Thanksgiving that brings families together.

# A Deep-Fried Thanksgiving

After Eric's turkey deep fryer lay dormant for many years, he let Brenda use it. This unexpected gift inspired them to write the following:

*It's on clearance, what a deal!*
*A turkey deep fryer to cook our Thanksgiving meal.*

*Just season to taste with spices and such*
*A pinch here and there, not too much.*
*But it says some assembly required*
*How to do it? I'm too tired.*
*Years go by and it sits on the shelf*
*Taunting me like an underutilized elf*
*Waiting to be used for the big holiday feast*
*Bothering my wife not in the least.*
*We should use it when the family's in town*
*But it's still not assembled, I feel so down.*

*Brenda asks how a deep fried turkey might cook*
*I'm eager to try it, let's have a look.*
*She says, "I have a smoker to offer in trade*
*For your turkey deep fryer unused for a decade*
*"No, the fryer is mine."*

*"But if you wanna use it, I guess that's fine."*
*Plans are made to break it in right*
*With special oil and a bird that won't fight.*
*The big day draws near, how will it go?*
*Without some experience, there is no way to know.*

*Family and friends arrive to see*
*How a Thanksgiving bird is cooked for free.*
*The oil is hot, ready at last*
*Keep the temperature steady to cook it fast.*
*Anticipation and laughter fill the air*
*As we wait anxiously for our Thanksgiving fare.*
*The turkey is cooked and ready to eat.*
*The glorious meal is crispy and neat.*
*Making for a mouth-watering display*
*A great way to spend Thanksgiving Day!*

You can view the one-minute YouTube video clips of how we prepared this turkey before it passed our lips. These fourteen video shorts show A to Z how fun cooking a turkey can be … maybe not for the turkey. Deep Fried Thanksgiving with friends and family at http://www.youtube.com/user/BrendaAvadian/videos.

# 25. Unexpected Gifts

As you diligently progress through each step in Part Four, you will be surprised by the unexpected gifts that will unveil themselves. These gifts remain unknown *until* you manage your clutter and appreciate what you find or learn in the process.

Sometimes these are tangible gifts—heirlooms, money, sentimental items, and other treasures. Other times, they are self-discoveries that free blocked pathways to your success, such as new ways of thinking.

Who would guess or even anticipate that after releasing a turkey deep fryer stored for a dozen years that the joy of discovery would bring families together for Thanksgiving?

Who could guess that between two books on a living room bookshelf was a packet containing $100,000 worth of U.S. Savings Bonds?

The gifts you find are unique to you. They unveil themselves only after you've gone through the process of getting your mind out of the clutter.

The return on your investment of time will exceed your expectations.

*How so?*

Explaining it is like trying to capture the multi-dimensional sensations of the world's most wondrous places with a two-dimensional image. At best, the image offers only a fraction of the experience, which doesn't mean we won't try to give you a sense of the unexpected gifts. Here are six:

- You will enjoy stronger relationships because you're more focused. You'll be less distracted and more attentive to the people you are with.

- You will think more clearly after removing the mental clutter that increases stress and cortisol levels, which cause weight gain and impair learning and memory.[15] It's as if a switch turns on in your mind to help you see and think more clearly.

- You will enjoy the fruits of creativity, nurtured by looking ahead as you reflect on where you've been. Ideas that would have never occurred to you when your mind was in the clutter will come to you.

- You won't accidentally donate or toss out something valuable, and you will properly dispose of anything that has the potential to cause harm.

- You will rekindle old relationships or regain clients when you take time to reconnect with people whose names you found in piles of old paperwork and in old emails.

- You will feel like a kid again. You will be more playful because you're not weighed down by all the things you must do.


*Well? What are you waiting for?*

With the ongoing practice of getting your mind out of the clutter, you will feel more confident to organize your life.

Sure, it's natural to question, What if I need this? What if it will be valuable someday?

Can your answers possibly justify the price you're paying now by holding onto too much stuff?

How about opening up space by letting go of a valued item you no longer need, only to receive an unexpected gift of even greater value? It doesn't happen all the time but when it does, wow!

Unexpected gifts rarely unfold while you're mired in piles, hoping you'll have the time or energy to sell your "valuable" stuff.

Our stuff is always worth more to us. (See *That's MINE!* in the Appendix.)

Your answer to "Do I need this *now?*" and actions in line with your response will help you organize your stuff in such a way to retrieve items more easily when you need them.

You need to focus on what's important to you *now.* Revisiting the first magic question will help with much of the stuff you are holding onto. *Will I take the time to acquire this item again if I lost it in a disaster?* If you are honest with yourself, the answer most often will be no.

# Donate to Enrich Self

Sometimes it's easier to get rid of your stuff if you know someone else will benefit. If you can't give it away to someone, donate it to a charity.

When you resist letting go because an item is worth a lot to you and you want to sell it, ask yourself if it's worth the time to plan, label, and display things for sale. Is it worth it to have strangers visit your home so they can bicker for even lower prices? What about the issue of safety when strangers visit your home?

The same goes for the hours that add up when you take pictures of your possessions, write a description, and then upload both to sell online. Is $100 or $200 worth the time, effort, and added stress?

*What is your time worth?*

## 25. Unexpected Gifts

When donating things in a meaningful way, two people benefit. By helping others with a donation or a gift, you affect someone else's life. Sometimes the unexpected gift you receive is learning just how much the thing you don't use any more means to someone else.

Remember how it feels after you do spring cleaning? Banished are all those pieces of lint on the carpet and dust bunnies scampering on your wood or tile floors. Your home looks brighter and smells fresher (yes, dust smells).

Like the first breath on a spring day after months of snow (for those who live in cold climates), we stretch out our arms, arch our back, take a deep breath, exhale, and smile.

When you clear out an area of clutter constipation, you feel relief. You feel the flow of life once more. You will be so satisfied you might want to host a party! *Which is crazy, because you'll have to clean all over again.*

But, who can resist celebrating such a monumental achievement with friends and family?

Not us!

*What are you waiting for?*

After you are finished getting your mind out of the clutter, help others who want to do the same. Remember when you started reading this book, how your clutter affected you? Share a copy with someone or use the BONUS *STUFFologist's Guide*.

# Afterword

Look around you. Can you even remember what your surroundings used to look like? Hopefully, you took before-and-after pictures to appreciate the difference resulting from your efforts.

How do you feel?

We hope you're smiling, because we are.

It starts with the first step, then the next. Sometimes, you will fall just like a toddler learning to take his first steps. Should you give up? No! With gentle encouragement, you will rise up again.

Besides, what better reason to celebrate than having less STUFF, and having time and space for the unexpected gifts that will come your way?

Yet, with every success comes a warning: Don't overdo it. There are plenty of gray areas. With physical clutter, it's not "Either I keep this to use or display or I get rid of it." If you obsessively get rid of too much, you may regret your actions, especially if you toss this book! ;-)

Our goal is to encourage you to strengthen the habits that have helped you get your mind out of the clutter. One way to reinforce your habits is to share what you've learned with others—to pay it forward.

We've created an easy-to-use tool to help you. The BONUS *STUFFologist's Guide* that follows is your quick start to help others get a handle on their stuff.

As you move forward in a clutter-free world, keep in mind Nature's cycle of input, throughput, and output. Remember this rule: **Free is not really free.**

Before you extend a hand to accept something for free (input), ask yourself the following:

*What will I do with it?*

*Where will I put it?*

*Do I have the space?*

*Will I use it?*

*How much time will it take?*

*Will I need to maintain (secure, repair, clean) it?*

*Will I be afraid that someone will take it?*

Your answers to these questions will determine how you spend your day (throughput and output).

Every day, each of us begins with the same amount of time. We have the power to choose how we spend that time.

*How will you spend your time?*

# BONUS STUFFologist's Guide

As longtime teachers, trainers, mentors, and advisors, we know that the best way to learn something is by helping someone else. *Ready?*

If you agree, we bestow upon you the title STUFFologist—one who has studied and applied fun and flexible approaches to getting rid of STUFF and wants to help others get their minds out of the clutter.

Who in your life is where you were when you decided to do something about your stuff? Is this person sick and tired of living amidst clutter?

Does s/he *want to* do something about it?

Is s/he *ready to* do something?

The answers to these last two questions are integral to your success. Without his/her desire, your efforts will be in vain. Without his/her readiness, you will grow flustered.

The *STUFFologist's Guide* is an easy-to-use tool to help you help others get their minds out of the clutter. The guide is organized using the acronym S.T.U.F.F.

To keep it personal, we've written this in the singular. To avoid using s/he and him/her, we'll alternate the gender for each letter of the acronym S.T.U.F.F.

# Start

Start by helping the person *define the clutter* in her life. What she defines as clutter will likely be different from your definition. Help her define her clutter by asking questions that not only address physical clutter (the most obvious) but also the other cluttergories that negatively affect our lives—mental, digital, temporal, and sensual.

To keep it manageable, start small—with the pile of mail on the counter or a catch-all box in the home office. Define clutter in one area at a time to avoid being overwhelmed. Even so, the person may hit a crisis point and need to stop. She may shout, "I want my life back!"—which is the response you're looking for before you'll be able to proceed. The first response (stopping) will require gentle encouragement and lots of patience.

In either situation, give her something to do to keep her commitment alive. Assign her an exercise *to write down her thoughts* about the clutter in her life or what else occupies her mind. Writing down thoughts will help her clear more mental clutter before taking the next step.

## Trust

Trust will be the cornerstone throughout this process. *Without* trust you won't get far.

Just as we gave you the opportunity to define *your* clutter and choose what you wanted to work on, you too must build and hold the person's trust by allowing him to guide you where he's ready to go.

Trust means gently pushing enough to make progress, which keeps his commitment alive and assures you that you're having an impact.

You must also trust that the steps you took to get your mind out of the clutter will help him do the same.

Encourage him to continue writing down his thoughts. Ask him to add a note or two about why he is holding onto a particular item, thought, or other cluttergory.

Let the person you're helping know that his notes are private and no one besides him will read them. This process of writing down thoughts helps get it out of his mind and onto paper (or on the computer) where he can look at the notes from a distance and with a more objective eye.

## Understand

Clutter builds up over time. Understand that getting rid of clutter will also take time. *How long did it take you?*

We view this as a process not an event.

Review Chapter 21 on input throughput output before helping the person understand Nature's cycle as it applies to getting her mind out of the clutter. This will give her confidence in your ability to help, while building trust in you.

Help her understand the importance of the first step of the six-step process by reminding her to define her clutter then to write down her thoughts. As she looks at her stuff, her definition of clutter may either narrow or expand.

As a STUFFologist, take time to understand where the person is coming from. Empathize. Do you remember how the process felt for you? You didn't want someone to rush you along or dictate what you should get rid of. When demands are made trust evaporates in an instant.

Instead, lead the way gently, as you allow her to set the pace. You've been through this while clearing your own clutter. Be patient and have compassion—two ingredients that will help her get unstuck, especially as this process unearths memories and emotions.

---

*Pay it forward—share what you've learned. Give the gift of STUFFology 101 to the person you're helping. Write an encouraging message inside and highlight the sections that were especially helpful to you.*

---

Understand that each item she tries to let go carries a host of memories, stories, and emotions. Needing to patiently listen and show compassion for the emotions that arise from these memories is as important to her as it was to you when you dealt with your clutter. Oftentimes, these stories and emotions produce obstacles to getting one's mind out of the clutter.

The Golden Rule applies here: Help the person deal with clutter with the same consideration you needed while dealing with yours.

Guide the person using the framework we offer here, which gives you ample flexibility.

## Focus

Clutter accumulates then overwhelms. Help the person *focus on doing one thing* at a time. Don't be tempted to work in too large of an area or in too many areas at once. You want him to be successful. If you focus on an area that takes an hour, his achievement will spur him to tackle the next area.

Finishing a small area is better than making partial progress on a larger one. An unfinished project does not spell "success" like a finished project does—however small.

We're driven to achieve. If there's too much in an area to accomplish, help him *dedicate a workspace* to focus only on what he puts in this workspace.

A small contained area is easier to deal with than an entire home or garage. Cleaning out a drawer in the kitchen or clearing off the workbench in the garage will have a better chance of yielding success.

Before-and-after photos can help fuel his drive to get his mind out of the clutter.

## Finish

With successful results, ask the person to define another area of clutter that she will process within a reasonable period of time.

You want her to *repeat small steps* and finish. Ongoing achievements build momentum and the motivation to continue getting her mind out of the clutter.

Follow up with her before your next visit to learn how she's doing and to encourage her to finish. She needs to *Do it NOW,* otherwise she'll lose motivation. Remember Newton's Second Law of Motion: A body in motion will remain in motion long enough to clear the clutter.

Helping the person define his/her clutter, write down thoughts, focus on doing one thing, dedicate a workspace, repeat small steps, and do it now will help him/her finish.

Sometimes, life gets in the way and despite all the motivation, progress slows or grinds to a halt. When this happens, reflect on your own journey and share what happened to you and what you did to regain momentum. Although your experience will be different from theirs, your support through each of the steps is what matters.

Remember, getting your mind out of the clutter is a process not an event. When a person suffers from clutter constipation, help him/her regain life's flow by assessing the importance of each possession in a specific area s/he defines as clutter. Asking the two magic questions will help.

---

*S.T.U.F.F.*
*Start*
*Trust*
*Understand*
*Focus*
*Finish*

---

# The Two Magic Questions

**Magic Question 1:** *Will you take time to acquire this item again if you lost it in a disaster?*

If the answer is no, the person has three options—donate or give away, dispose, or sell.

If the answer is yes, the person also has three options—set it aside to deal with later, display it, or use it.

Ask Magic Question 1 for each item in this focused area.

Despite our efforts to succeed, especially when we're close to achieving our goals, it seems life sabotages our efforts. *Ever run a mile or ten then feel you can't go on near the end?* The truth is we sabotage our own achievement. Perhaps, pointing the finger elsewhere prevents us from growing discouraged. Taking time to ponder our response to the second magic question will help us reach the finish line.

**Magic Question 2:** *What would the area I'm focusing on now look, feel, smell, or sound like if I cleared out the clutter?*

To help the person visualize this, share your experiences or those we've included in Part Three and in the *Unexpected Gifts* chapter. For us, these mean peace of mind, bringing families together, financial windfall, and being able to play a game of pool. They also include no need to contort to reach what we need in the home office while enjoying less stress after finding things easily. Additional benefits are clean countertops, being able to eat at the kitchen table, opening the door to an unexpected guest without having to clean, and paying bills on time.

With this *STUFFologist's Guide*, you will be sure to help others take steps to get their minds out of the clutter.

Celebrate small steps along the way. Have a cheering session virtually or raise a glass to offer a toast in-person. When your family and friends achieve success, celebrate together, and then pay it forward.

*Who knows? One day, you may lead an army of STUFFologists ready to battle clutter around the world!*

# Acknowledgments

As with any endeavor, there are those who touched our lives, offered ideas, and helped shape *STUFFology 101*.

Many people have woven themselves into the fabric of our lives. Some include: Patrick Arbore, Mary Barrass, Lee Berghtold, Marilyn Bell, Bruce and Karla Borden, Chris de la Torre, Sharon Goldinger, Jo Guidry, Sally Howard, Louise Levin, Lew Jurey, Maggie McNamara, Karen Ostler, Kathy Parenteau, David and Sharon Price, William and Margaret Riddle, Lois Rose Rose, Susanne Rossi, and Karen Smeltzer.

There are those whose lives we touched as a result of our own combined eight decades of experience getting our minds out of the clutter.

Thank you, fellow Toastmasters from High Desert, Platinum Speakers, and Pro Talk clubs in Division A of District 33, for supporting us throughout this endeavor: Nannette Barrie, Zanya Biviano, Nancy Burroughs, Dave and Leona Byrne, Vince Carter, Greg Crawley, Brenda Fenner, Betsy Haslett, Charles Heydon, Celia

Hurdle, Ann Hill, Dennis Kneer, Miguel Mayorga, Ken Mitchell, Al Nelson, Judi Olson, Mayra Padilla, and Dave Sauer.

We thank Mary Jo Zazueta who edited our manuscript so that we could deliver our message more concisely and clearly.

Thank you, Julia Ryan, for designing a world-class cover that conveys our fun and flexible approach to help people *get their minds out of the clutter*.

Thank you, Mayapriya Long, for creating a playful whimsical design for the interior of *STUFFology 101*.

Finally, and most importantly, we thank our families who supported us by sharing ideas and serving as examples. They picked up our share of responsibilities at home, while we devoted over a 1,000 hours during all-day weekend sessions, hours-long weekday and weekend phone calls, in order to distill our knowledge and experiences into the pages that became *STUFFology 101*.

Thank you, David Borden, Susan Riddle, Jackie Riddle, Douglas Thoin, Beth Riddle Harmon, and Maggie Riddle.

# Appendix
# That's MINE!

To better understand the first magic question, picture two children screaming, "That's MINE!" while in a tug-of-war over a toy.

"The Endowment Effect" is when we want to hold onto something because it is already in our possession. Once we have it, it's hard to let go.

Studies show that once an item is ours, the perceived value of the item increases.

If it's so hard to let go of something we already own, what if we say no more often? Saying no is much easier than trying to let go of something we have; although getting something free is awfully tempting.

## The Endowment Effect

Psychologist Daniel Kahneman and a team of researchers studied the endowment effect among college students.[16, 17, 18] Half were given a mug featuring the university's emblem and half were given cash. The psychologists expected the students to trade cash for mugs and vice versa but few were willing to give up their mugs. The students who were given the mugs placed a higher value on them than the students with cash were willing to pay.

Even professionals who study this stuff find it hard to let go.

Tom Stafford, lecturer in Psychology and Cognitive Science for the Department of Psychology at the University of Sheffield England initially attempted to get rid of his stuff and failed.[19] He came up with a reason to keep each item. To be successful, the next time he tried, he unknowingly employed an *anti-endowment effect strategy*. He states: *[K]nowing the power of the bias, for each item I ask myself a simple question: If I didn't have this, how much effort would I put in to obtain it? And then more often or not I throw it away, concluding that if I didn't have it, I wouldn't want this.*

Like Tom Stafford, answering the first magic question will help you be more rational when valuing what you already own. For more about valuing what you own, read Elizabeth O'Brien's, "10 things estate sales won't tell you."[20]

# Notes

## Chapter 1

[1] George Carlin. *Stuff* (video). Comedy sketch includes the late George Carlin's insights on stuff including his definition: *A house is just a pile of stuff with a cover on it.* Length: 5 minutes Content Age 17 or above.
http://www.youtube.com/watch?v=MvgN5gCuLac

[2] Randy O. Frost and Gail Steketee. *Stuff: Compulsive Hoarding and the Meaning of Things* (Houghton Mifflin Harcourt, 2010). Addresses the psychological aspects of hoarding and why things are important to us or "Why stuff matters."

[3] *Diagnostic and Statistical Manual of Mental Disorders Fifth Edition (DSM-5)* (American Psychiatric Association, 2013). Lists hoarding as a separate condition; although it can also be a symptom of other disorders such as Obsessive Compulsive Disorder (OCD), depression, and grief. A good article to learn more about Hoarding Disorder at HD

or Hoarding Disorder defined by the American Psychiatric Association including diagnosing, risk factors, and treatment options.

http://www.psychiatry.org/hoarding-disorder

http://www.psychiatry.org/practice/dsm/dsm5/dsm-5-video-series-hoarding-disorder

## Chapter 2

[4] *Zen: The Path of Meditation* Scroll below video to learn what is Zen Buddhism, Zen beliefs and practices, and different schools of Zen Buddhism.

http://www.religionfacts.com/buddhism/sects/zen.htm

[5] Marina City condominium image in Chicago

http://www.flickr.com/photos/43522727@N05/4048112634/

## Chapter 3

[6] "The Station Fire"

http://inciweb.nwcg.gov/incident/1856/

[7] Brenda Avadian. "The Station Fire" adapted from "FIRE! Quick! What really matters?" by Brenda Avadian, 2010

http://thecaregiversvoice.com/latest-news/fire-quick-what-really-matters/

## Chapter 4

[8] Brenda Avadian. "The Wooden Spoon" adapted from an award-winning presentation delivered at the 2008 District 33 Toastmasters Conference.

## Chapter 9

[9] Brenda Avadian. "The Toy Gun that Killed" adapted from article posted at TheCaregiversVoice.com on October 27th, 2010.
http://thecaregiversvoice.com/latest-news/the-toy-gun-that-killed/

## Chapter 11

[10] Brenda Avadian. Based on "Scoop Up Piles of Overwhelming Paperwork" EzineArticles.com
http://EzineArticles.com/6793182

[11] Dr. Audri Lanford and Jim. Paperitis.com offers productivity tips and articles to reduce paper clutter.

## Chapter 14

[12] Marla Cilley. (aka: FlyLady) Links to "What is FlyLady?" page for housecleaning and organizing tips with humor.
http://www.flylady.net/d/what-is-flylady/

## Chapter 22

[13] See "That's MINE!" in Appendix for more information about Tom Stafford's work at the University of Sheffield with The Endowment Effect.

## Chapter 24

[14] Brenda Avadian. "The U.S. Savings Bond Windfall," *"Where's my shoes?" My Father's Walk through Alzheimer's 2nd edition* (North Star Books, 2005).

## Chapter 25

[15] *Stress: Chronic stress puts your health at risk* (Mayo Clinic staff). Includes understanding natural stress response and the health problems that occur when stress response goes haywire.
http://www.mayoclinic.org/healthy-living/stress-management/in-depth/stress/art-20046037

## Appendix

[16] Daniel Kahneman, Jack L. Knetsch, and Richard H. Thaler. "Experimental Tests of the Endowment Effect and the Coase Theorem," *Journal of Political Economy Vol. 98, No. 6* (University of Chicago Press, December 1990), pp. 1325-1348
http://www.jstor.org/discover/10.2307/2937761

[17] —"Anomalies: The Endowment Effect, Loss Aversion, and Status Quo Bias," *The Journal of Economic*

*Perspectives Vol. 5, No. 1* (Winter, 1991), pp. 193-206 American Economic Association Article http://www.jstor.org/stable/1942711

[18] Pat Jeffries. "Clutter tip of the week: Ask better questions to overcome the 'endowment effect,'" *The Oregonian* (August 19, 2012).
http://www.oregonlive.com/hg/index.ssf/2012/08/clutter_tip_of_the_week_ask_be.html

[19] Tom Stafford. "Why we love to hoard...and how you can overcome it." *BBC Future* (July 17, 2012).
http://www.bbc.com/future/story/20120717-why-we-love-to-hoard

[20] Elizabeth O'Brien. "10 things estate sales won't tell you," *Market Watch* (June 19, 2013).
http://www.marketwatch.com/story/10-things-estate-sales-wont-tell-you-2013-06-14

# Additional Resources

*The following include additional resources to get your mind out of the clutter. When posting links to articles online, we take a risk. In the event the URL has changed, please search using the words in the title.*

**Avadian, Brenda.** "HOARDING Things: How to Stop," TheCaregiversVoice.com, March 2010.

http://www.thecaregiversvoice.com/
latest-news/hoarding-things-how-to-stop/

How-to article offering strategies for caregivers to help loved ones stop hoarding. Practical advice with specific solutions to issues faced by a caregiver for someone with cognitive impairment.

**Carver, Courtney.** "On All the Sentimental Stuff and Clutter," BeMoreWithLess.com, 2013.

http://bemorewithless.com/heartstuff/

Provides questions to ask when deciding on which sentimental clutter items to keep, toss, or donate.

**Coker, Carmen.** *7 days to a More Organized You,* LessonsFromOrganizing.com, 2012.

Coker's 15-page booklet offers one tip for each day of the week to handle six types of clutter, some of which overlap with the cluttergories in *STUFF-ology 101*.

**Fake, Caterina.** "How to Create Time," October 2, 2012.

http://www.linkedin.com/today/post/article/20121002125913-3279-how-to-create-time

Practical advice in six steps about how to make time in your day.

**Jeffries, Pat.** "Clutter tip of the week: A roundup of useful advice and intriguing info," *The Oregonian,* October 21, 2012.

http://www.oregonlive.com/hg/index.ssf/2012/10/clutter_tip_of_the_week_a_roun.html

Addresses paper versus digital clutter; hoarding versus being messy, storing things in our cars, and touches on dementia.

**Kotz, Deborah.** "Feeling overwhelmed by clutter? 7 stress-reducing tips," Daily Dose at Boston.com, August 8, 2012.

http://www.boston.com/dailydose/2012/08/09/feeling-overwhelmed-clutter-stress-reducing-tips/GeQVkjmxHyPMW0BhAvpsSM/story.html

Explains how clutter causes stress and anxiety. Offers seven tips to eliminate stress. Based on the UCLA study and book, *Life at Home in the 21st Century*, which looks at the physiological impact of clutter.

**Lindquist, Shannon.** Too much clutter in your house = too much clutter in your head, Michigan State University Extension, August 2, 2013.

http://msue.anr.msu.edu/news/too_much_clutter_in_your_house_too_much_clutter_in_your_head

"Clutter takes up space in your house and your head. It has a hold on you every day. Find out how to free space in your home and clear your mind at the same time."

**McPherson, Patty.** "GOT CLUTTER? The 10 commandments of decluttering," *Wicked Local*, October 7, 2012.

http://www.wickedlocal.com/x1711843004/GOT-CLUTTER-The-10-commandments-of-decluttering#axzz29ureD8DW

A light-hearted take on clearing the clutter in your home.

**Morrero, Lorie.** *The Clutter Diet*, Reason Press, 2009. Morrero's website offers more information.

http://www.clutterdietblog.com/

Helpful how-to video tips for dealing with clutter http://www.youtube.com/user/clutterdiet.

**Palmer, Brooks.** *Clutter Busting,* New World Library, 2009.

Addresses clutter as "anything in your life that doesn't serve you" and helps you feel better when you let go.

**Palmer, Brooks.** *Clutter Busting Your Life,* New World Library, 2012.

Takes clutter to the next level—how clutter affects your relationship with yourself and others.

**Sholl, Jessie.** "The Emotional Toll of Clutter," ExperienceLife.com, April 2013.

http://experiencelife.com/article/ the-emotional-toll-of-clutter/

How clutter affects our lives on an emotional level starting with a real-life example. Addresses broader clutter-management topics.

**Taylor, Jim.** "De-Clutter Your Life!" *Huffington Post,* August 10, 2012.

http://www.huffingtonpost.com/dr-jim-taylor/ declutter_b_1748165.html

Actionable tips to de-clutter your life, including less temporal clutter.

**Tolin, David F.; Frost, Randy O.; and Sketekee, Gail.** *Buried in Treasures: Help for Compulsive Acquiring, Saving and Hoarding,* Oxford University Press, 2007. Also refer to "Photos: Are you a Hoarder" in the *Sun Sentinel.*

http://www.sun-sentinel.com/health/ sfl-hoarder-levels-pictures-20120706,0,3751767. photogallery

These 27 images courtesy of Oxford University Press (July 6, 2012) detail the continuum from clutter to hoarding in a bedroom.

**Walsh, Peter.** "Ten Ways to Declutter Your Home," Oprah.com, February 7, 2007.

http://www.oprah.com/home/Peter- Walshs-10-Tips-to-De-Clutter-Your-Home

A quick 10-point checklist. Additional informative links available under the "Keep Reading" section on this web page.

# Index

## D

## E

## F

# Index

# Index

# About Your STUFFologists

 **Brenda Avadian, MA,** has been dealing with clutter since age eight—that's forty-six years. "I've struggled with letting go," she says. "I've tried over the years to let go of things, but what if I need to refer to that 1970's *National Geographic* article on Yugoslavian protocol?"

The author of nine books, Brenda has had a varied career, including working as a university professor, executive coach, corporate consultant, caregiver, and national speaker.

She traveled nearly 2,000 miles to clear out her parents' home—filled with her father's collection of "spare parts for everything" and all the free stuff her mother amassed after saying yes so many times when she should have been saying no.

"It amazes me what occupies our lives. We come into this world with nothing. We leave this world with nothing. Yet we spend a significant amount of our lives with things," she says.

It wasn't until Brenda began caring for her father and going through his paperwork that an eighty-five-year-old sage's question got her thinking and taking steps toward getting her mind out of the clutter:

"Where do you want to spend your time, with *things* or with *people*?"

**Eric Riddle** has been a lifelong packrat. His mantra has been: I would rather have it and not need it than need it and not have it.

Since age eleven, he's been dealing with his parents' clutter and his own—that's thirty-seven years. Eric knew what he had to do. He just had to do it.

Working in customer service and sales has given Eric a deeper view of human nature. He understands, given all the mental and temporal clutter in our lives, that our concerns demand unique answers.

Eric believes clutter is a reflection of life. Recent events led Eric to face the clutter in his own life with a new perspective.

- After his eldest daughter, Jackie, moved out of the house eight years ago and got married, she returned home to clear out her bedroom. Eric realized then that his home didn't need to be a storage unit for his grown children.

- Eric learned how to keep things cleaner and better organized after his middle daughter, Beth, applied what she learned in the Army during visits home, before getting married.

- When his wife, Susan, and youngest daughter, Maggie, needed the pool table to practice for a cancer fundraiser, the whole family stepped in to clear the clutter.

Getting your mind out of the clutter is an ongoing process. Eric's experiences in the land of STUFF have him moving farther away from clutter toward clarity.

# We Want to Hear From You

## We invite you to tell your story.

- *How did a copy of* STUFFology 101 *come into your life?*
- *Describe your situation with STUFF when you began reading this book.*
- *In what area(s) did you succeed in getting your mind out of the clutter?*
- *Did you use what you learned to help someone else?*

Send your story with before-and-after pictures to SUCCESS@STUFFology101.com

Be sure to include your name and telephone number so we can follow up with you if necessary.

We will request your permission first if we decide to feature your story on STUFFology101.com, use an excerpt as a testimonial, or use your story for inclusion in an upcoming book.

# We're Here to Serve You

- *Want more?*
- *Want to walk this road with an experienced STUFFologist?*
- *Did you try something that didn't work?*
- *Want to feel less pain getting your mind out of the clutter?*

We offer **STUFFology 101 mentoring** to keep your mind out of the clutter. Our Gold Package includes six biweekly phone calls to help you define your clutter and discover breakthrough solutions to relieve your clutter constipation.

We'll follow up with three monthly calls.

Finally, during two quarterly calls, we'll celebrate and anchor your success.

This Gold Package offer is limited to fifty clients per year. We also offer Silver and Bronze packages for smaller STUFF.

Send us an email at HELP@STUFFology101.com

*The other side of clutter is clarity*

CPSIA information can be obtained at www.ICGtesting.com
Printed in the USA
LVOW01s1504190415

435210LV00018BA/1262/P